Monographs

of the Rutgers Center of Alcohol Studies

No. 4

Monographs of the
Rutgers Center of Alcohol Studies

Under the editorship of Mark Keller

This monograph series was begun as "Monographs of the Yale Center of Alcohol Studies" and Numbers 1, 2 and 3 were published at Yale. Beginning with this monograph the series will be continued as the Monographs of the Rutgers Center of Alcohol Studies. The change conforms with the transfer of the Center from Yale to Rutgers University. The works published in this series report the results of original research in any of the scientific disciplines, whether performed at Rutgers or elsewhere.

No. 1. Alcohol and the Jews. A Cultural Study of Drinking and Sobriety. By CHARLES R. SNYDER. $5.00

No. 2. Revolving Door. A Study of the Chronic Police Case Inebriate. By DAVID J. PITTMAN and C. WAYNE GORDON. $4.00

No. 3. Alcohol in Italian Culture. Food and Wine in Relation to Sobriety among Italians and Italian Americans. By GIORGIO LOLLI, EMIDIO SERIANNI, GRACE M. GOLDER and PIERPAOLO LUZZATTO-FEGIZ. $4.00

No. 4. Drinking among Teen-Agers. A Sociological Interpretation of Alcohol Use by High-School Students. By GEORGE L. MADDOX and BEVODE C. MCCALL. $6.00

No. 5. Drinking in French Culture. By ROLAND SADOUN, GIORGIO LOLLI and MILTON SILVERMAN. In press.

Drinking among Teen-Agers

Distributed by

College & University Press · *Publishers*

263 Chapel Street   New Haven, Conn.

Drinking among Teen-Agers

A Sociological Interpretation of Alcohol Use
by High-School Students

BY

George L. Maddox, Ph.D.

Professor of Medical Sociology, Duke University

AND

Bevode C. McCall, Ph.D.

Associate Professor of Sociology, Wayne State University

PUBLICATIONS DIVISION
RUTGERS CENTER OF ALCOHOL STUDIES
NEW BRUNSWICK NEW JERSEY

Library of Congress catalog card number: 64-63392

MANUFACTURED IN THE UNITED STATES OF AMERICA BY
UNITED PRINTING SERVICES, INC.
NEW HAVEN, CONN.

Contents

List of Tables

Acknowledgments

The authors are indebted to many individuals whose encouragement and help made the publication of this research possible. A very special debt to John Useem, currently Chairman of the Department of Sociology and Anthropology, Michigan State University, is gratefully acknowledged. He was a persistent critic as he read various drafts of the manuscript, but always a friendly critic.

Several colleagues also deserve special recognition for their contributions in conceptualizing, administering and implementing the Teen-Age Drinking Project within the framework of the Social Research Service, Michigan State University. We acknowledge especially the contributions of Charles P. Loomis, Director of the Social Research Service; of Gregory P. Stone, now of the University of Minnesota; and of Christopher Sower, Michigan State University.

Ralph Daniel, Executive Director, Michigan State Board of Alcoholism, initially was a proponent of research on drinking patterns among teenagers and was a dependable advocate of the research group before his Board. The members of his Board have proved to be generous and patient men. Mr. Daniel's continuing support has been invaluable.

A grant-in-aid from the Graduate Research Council, University of Missouri, which made possible certain parts of the data analysis, is gratefully acknowledged. The assistance of Don Spencer, a graduate student in the Department of Sociology, University of Missouri, was made possible by this grant.

The cooperation of high-school administrators and students, who remain unnamed, was the sine qua non of the research. Within the limits which the school administrators felt it was necessary to set, our reception was cordial and our access to the students was expedited. The friendly acceptance by the students was all we could have asked.

While many people encouraged and helped us, the limitations of this study are ours alone. We can only thank our friends for helping to keep our errors to a minimum.

Introduction

THE OLDER LITERATURE on the problem of youth drinking is more voluminous than anyone can imagine. Physicians and biologists, clergymen and social reformers, as well as educators, are joined with a host of civic officials and devoted temperance workers in discussions of this topic. Whether they declaim with alarm, offer good advice, warn of specific dangers, or propose schemes for hopefully effective instruction, all agree on one thing: the young should not drink beverages containing alcohol. Occasionally some reports of systematic study appear. The health status or intelligence of children who drink, or the crime records of their parents, may be compared with the same thing in children who don't—generally to the advantage of the abstinent youngsters. There are even a few attempts to measure the actual state of affairs with respect to drinking or alcoholism among children, though sometimes the investigators do not distinguish between the two.

The gross naiveté of much of this older literature is matched only by its sincerity and repetitiveness. If the beginning of the present century is taken as a starting point, after 25 or 30 years a new generation of educators and reformers, with their allies in the temperance movement and in science, will be found making the same statements about dangers, and the same proposals for intensified education (sometimes frankly identified as propaganda). If the activity temporarily wanes in one country, it gains new impetus in another; and in the periodic International Congresses (against alcohol, or against alcoholism) this cause will always receive abundant report. Here, indeed, countries otherwise rarely heard from will be represented by those concerned with the dangers of alcohol for youth. It is tempting to think that these worriers must have succeeded in their temperance aims—as otherwise the threatened dysgenetic effects of alcoholized youth should have overwhelmed at least the United States, Germany, France and Russia, but many other countries as well. The difficulty in accepting this conclusion is that the same concern about youth drinking is still being expressed by the present generation of adults, and the contemporary evidence confirms that youth drinking is a fact.

Education about alcohol—literally propaganda about the evil effects of alcohol—was legally required in most of the primary or secondary school systems of the United States when Anne Roe initiated a new look at this subject in the early 1940's. At about the same time some educators and sociologists began to examine the actual situation of drinking by youngsters attending the school systems, and the results—the substantial percentages of adolescents who affirmed that they had been initiated into drinking—were surprising. An interesting by-discovery was the claim, by a large proportion of the boys and girls, that much of their drinking was done at home with parental permission. But there was also a good deal of clandestine drinking by the children of nonpermissive parents—very often the children of parents who preached not as they did.

An outstanding feature of the older youth-drinking literature is the unconscious alienation of the authors from the subjects of their concern—the young people. Clearly they stood on a high platform, imbued with noble intentions, and viewed what youth did, and pronounced what youth ought to do, and devised what youth should be taught, without any manifest concern for what the young people themselves thought or how they felt about it all. The authorities were satisfied with their knowledge of what the young ought to think and do. On the evidence of the actual drinking behaviors produced by the surveys in American high schools and colleges in the past 20 years, the abstinence propaganda passed off as education in the schools in the preceding half century must have failed. Where abstinence prevails it seems to be related to traditional family practice, often religiously oriented. This is not to say that, where there was an abstinence tradition, the evils-of-alcohol teachings did not have a reinforcing effect. Also, in communities without an abstinence tradition, the failure of the evils-of-alcohol teachings cannot be demonstrated—it can only be guessed—for there is much to indicate that the required teaching was perfunctory when not altogether neglected. But on the whole, when one considers the enormous effort put into teaching youth the evil effects of drinking during several successive generations, and when one adds to this the nearly universal legislative prohibition of the sale and purchase, sometimes also of the drinking, of alcoholic beverages by those aged under 21, and when this is compared with the actual behavior of the majority of adolescents as discovered in recent years, then the gap between what adults want and what young people do is astronomical.

Clearly this is an attractive field for social scientists concerned with problems of child rearing, problems of education, problems of youth culture, problems of intergenerational relationship, problems of the transmission of social values, problems of socialization.

Surely a further new look is required. Surely it is time for adults to ask themselves, and to face the questions realistically, about what they truly want and expect of youth. Do the majority of adults in nearly all of the states in this country really expect young people to refrain from drinking any alcoholic beverage until their 21st birthday? Even if they go to work? Even if they go into the Army, Navy and Air Force? Even if they get married and become parents? And if the adults do not demand so much, but are prepared to recognize that most young people will sometimes drink before they are 21—quite many, long before—then under what circumstances, with what preparation, would they prefer to have the drinking mores learned, and the drinking done? For one thing is certain: All those who have been worried about youth drinking, and concerned to prevent it, have not been merely naive. Indeed they have had good cause; for drinking can be very dangerous for adults, and especially for youth.

If the adults of this generation should be prepared to exhibit the maturity and wisdom to face the problems of youth drinking realistically, then they must first have a body of knowledge and a basis for understanding on which rational policies can be projected. It is too easy, for example, to jump to the conclusion that, because Italian and Jewish children are introduced to wine early, and these groups have low rates of alcohol-related pathologies, therefore the solution is early initiation of all children into drinking. We do not know definitively why certain groups are comparatively immune to alcohol problems, and the early initiation of drinking may be a mere coincidence, and could be disastrous in other groups lacking the real basis of immunity. Moreover, there seem to be populations with early introduction of children to drinking, who do not lack alcohol pathologies, including alcoholism. It may well be that in many groups the postponement of drinking until adulthood—and for some, permanent abstinence—is the decisive preventive of alcohol-related catastrophe.

The requisite body of knowledge is in process of development.

One essential part of it already exists in good measure: this is information about actual youth drinking behavior. Another essential part is in the making: this is information on the attitudes, the beliefs, the thinking of young people about drinking—their own drinking and the drinking by adults—and about not drinking.

The present book constitutes an important contribution to both these classes of knowledge. It reports on the drinking practices of nearly 2,000 adolescents in a midwestern American community. But more importantly, it reports on, and analyzes with refreshing sophistication, the thinking of these young people about their behavior. Thus, for example, it reveals the fascinating distinction that many adolescents make in classifying themselves as nondrinkers at the same time that they report themselves as drinkers. In their analysis, Maddox and McCall have chosen to compare not merely boys and girls who do and don't drink, but also, as a third class, those who say they drink but choose to call themselves not-drinkers.

But the chief merit of this work lies actually beyond the excellent review of previous knowledge, the contribution of new data, and the analysis of the new material. It lies in the interpretation of the data, in the presentation of a theoretical basis for their comprehension. In placing the revealed facts about youth attitudes on drinking and abstinence within a framework of social science theory, Maddox and McCall have in effect challenged the relevant disciplines—sociology, educational psychology, political science—to come to grips with the issues discussed above.

The hiatus between the practices of those who, on the approach to adulthood, are experimenting with adult roles, and the wishes of those who have achieved the authority of adult status, is no small matter. With the possible exception of sex relations, there is no area of behavior in which intergenerational conflict is so obvious, and yet so beclouded by misunderstanding, as in drinking. By shedding light on youth's side of the issue, the authors of this work have made a beginning at dispersing the dust-clouds and thus terminating one of the chief causes of misunderstanding. Adults who attend to the facts and the interpretation here provided should become better able to cope with the youth-drinking problem—and perhaps also with other problems in the rearing and preparation of the upcoming generation for its adult responsibilities.

This book, then, like many alcohol-related studies, is of interest and has significance far beyond its immediate subject matter. Of course its content and its ideas will be useful to all who are directly concerned with the rearing of youth—educators, the clergy, the temperance advocates, and the legislators and civic officers who may decree what shall be permitted or prohibited, or even what shall be taught. But more still, it merits the serious consideration of the intellectual community to which society must look for the theoretical and logical basis of rational public policies.

It would not be hard to show that this work has, besides great merits, also a measure of flaws and weaknesses. For example, much was lost by the failure to elicit information about sex behavior and religious affiliation. The decision to avoid these areas was made by the school administrators whose cooperation in the conduct of the study was essential. The authors, in retrospect, feel that the caution of the officials was justified. On the touchy subject of sex, and given the particular time and circumstances of the study, one would not want to argue the point. At any rate, the lack is only in additional information. On the subject of religion, however, it is unavoidable to feel that the school officials were in error. The argument that bigots sometimes misuse religiously identified data is pusillanimous. The amount of social science data on religious groups is now monumental, and is religiously ignored by bigots, who have neither need for nor interest in data. Unfortunately here the lack of information interferes with the most effective analysis of the data, and at some points renders the interpretation dubious. Regrettable, too, is the choice of procedure which made it necessary to tabulate much of the data in what seems to this reader a topsy-turvy arrangement. Thus, for example, Table 10 tells what percentage of those who are drinkers, self-styled nondrinkers, and actual nondrinkers are aged 16 or less, 17, or 18 plus, instead of telling what percentage of each age are drinkers, nondrinkers and nonusers. This defect, however, is remedied in the text for many important categories of information.

In spite of these and other faults, which critical readers will profitably discover, the work here presented begins to clarify the process whereby drinking or not drinking becomes integrated with the behavior of American adolescents, and suggests how this behavior becomes associated with the aspirations of youth for adult status. It is thus the most important work of the present generation on the subject of youth drinking.

It often happens in social science that the findings which emerge from a study seem obvious. Anti-intellectual boors sometimes attempt to show off their superiority by pointing out that only academicians needed a formal study to discover what everybody with an ounce of horse sense knew all along. In the present case there is some danger that the authors' ultimate conclusion—that adolescents do not have to invent the idea of drinking, that they learn it—may seem all too obvious. The assertion of great importance for this work may then also seem rather exaggerated. Yet the adult community has for many generations treated drinking by youth precisely as if it were something that youngsters repeatedly invent anew, and which they should and can be persuaded to treat as an alien phenomenon. This unrealistic wish to divorce adolescent behavior from adult example is old and deeply rooted, and only its exposure by means of formal study and scientific methodology has a chance to influence the adult authorities to dare a fresh approach. Therein, as is often the case with studies in the social sciences, lies the importance of this work for the welfare of society. Only time can confirm or confound this prediction. But in the meantime this work is sure to set many minds to thinking.

MARK KELLER

Chapter 1

TEEN-AGERS AND ALCOHOL

ADOLESCENTS typically fascinate adults. The teen-ager, who is no longer a child but not quite an adult, is fascinating primarily because he is a mirror in which the adult may see an extension of himself. The teen-ager is a living commentary on the generation that rears him and a prophecy about the generation that will inherit the future. Adults in every society, therefore, have a tremendous emotional as well as practical investment in the adolescent's success in making the transition from childhood to adulthood. Every society stakes its life on the assumption that he will be trained so as to become a competent and responsible member of some community.

With such high stakes involved it should not be surprising that adults in our society periodically appraise the state of the adolescent's health, his education, or any real or imagined indication of his competence or responsibility. Nor is it surprising that a generation of adults in our society, which numbers its alcoholics and the cost of its excesses with beverage alcohol in the multiple millions, periodically looks with some apprehension at what adolescents say about and do with alcohol. For years now parents, ministers, educators, legislators, editorialists and civic officials have exercised their legitimate right to guess, but with undetermined accuracy, about teen-age attitudes toward drinking and about their drinking behavior. There has always been disagreement whether young people should be indicted for a too realistic imitation of adult drinking behavior or commended for not imitating that behavior.

There is still room for argument whether young people should be praised or blamed for what they think about and do with alcohol. Research is making it increasingly less necessary, however, to guess about what they are thinking and doing, at least as far as the teen-ager in high school is concerned.

The research to be reported here is an account of what almost 2,000 teen-agers in the eleventh and twelfth grades of 3 public high schools in a middle-sized midwestern city a few years ago reported they were thinking about and doing with beverage alcohol. The teen-agers in this single community do not represent all adolescents or even the adolescents in public schools. Yet knowledge of their attitudes toward and their use and nonuse of alcohol should contribute to a better understanding of the process by which the abstinence typical of childhood is more often than not transformed into the drinking behavior typical of the majority of adults in our society and particularly of the process by which many adolescents eventually not only use alcohol but also come to include its use as an integral part of their self-image.

This investigation of the part which alcohol plays in the life of the adolescent was initiated and financed by the Michigan Board of Alcoholism. It was planned and carried out by sociologists in the Social Research Service, Michigan State University.

The Sample and The Method[1]

A pretested questionnaire was used to explore what teen-agers in the public high schools in one community were thinking about and doing with beverage alcohol and also to explore their peer relationships, their identification with the culture and social system of the high school, the social roles which were most meaningful to them, and the inclusion or exclusion of alcohol use as an integral part of their self-image and style of life. The questionnaire is reproduced in Appendix II. All the students attending each of the 3 high schools were assembled on a given day and the purpose of the research was explained to them. Anonymity was assured both by research personnel and school officials and a reasonable procedure for securing that anonymity was described. Of all the students enrolled in the 3 schools, 1,962 (95 per cent) satisfactorily completed the questionnaire. Indications of noncooperation warranting rejection of questionnaires were few.

For purposes of analysis the students were placed in three categories: *(1)* those who indicated they were users of beverage alcohol (that is, their exposure to alcohol involved more than a single, isolated experimental drink or taste) and who identified themselves as "drinkers"; *(2)* those who indicated that they were users but did not choose to identify themselves as "drinkers"; and *(3)* those who neither indicated that they were users nor chose to identify themselves as "drinkers."

[1] For notes on methods and procedures, see Appendix I.

There were 177 teen-agers who identified themselves as "drinkers" and reported using beverage alcohol; an additional 279 students who did not consider themselves as "drinkers" nonetheless reported patterns of alcohol use which clearly indicated they were not abstinent. All 456 of the students in these two categories, 23.2% of the total, were used subsequently in the analysis. Since resources did not permit coding the responses of the remaining 1,506 nonusers or abstinent students (those who neither reported a pattern of alcohol use nor identified themselves as "drinkers"), a 17.3% random sample was drawn from this group. Experience has shown that, on the basis of a random sample of this size, reasonably accurate inferences about the abstaining teen-agers in this study may be drawn.[2]

After the survey questionnaires had been completed, 55 students were chosen on a random basis for intensive interviewing. These interviews lasted about 1 hour, were tape recorded, and later transcribed verbatim. These interviews were designed to provide a check on the reliability of the questionnaire responses and to give depth, detail and coherence to the precoded answers used in the questionnaires. The meaning of responses could be probed, elaboration and details requested. Reassured of anonymity, the students selected showed little reluctance either to being interviewed or to giving "for instances" of their feeling about or the uses of alcohol by themselves and their peers.

This report is admittedly not about teen-agers in general or even about teen-agers in Michigan. Rather it is a report on the teen-agers in the public high schools of a middle-sized midwestern community. This community had a population of slightly over 92,000 in 1950 and was part of a standard metropolitan area with a population of about 173,000. Although not necessarily a typical community in Michigan, it was not very different from other urban communities in Michigan in its rate of growth, the median income of its citizens, or the socioeconomic, racial and ethnic composition of its population.

The Proposition

The proposition developed from the evidence gathered in this research is this: Young people do not invent the idea that they

[2] For a general discussion of random sampling procedure and statistical inference, see Hagood, M. J. and Price, D. O. Statistics for Sociologists (rev. ed.); Ch. 17. New York; Holt; 1952.

should drink (or abstain); they learn it. The acceptability and desirability of some drinking behavior is continually suggested to a young person by the elaborate integration of alcohol use with North American culture and adult social behavior. A majority of adults in the United States drink at least sometimes; it is likely that the proportion of drinkers (about two out of three) and the drinking patterns of adults have remained relatively stable for the past two decades. Children, on the other hand, are generally assumed to be abstinent. Any attempt to explain the persistence of adult drinking behavior necessarily focuses attention on when and how the abstinence of childhood is transformed for the majority into the drinking behavior of adulthood.

The when and how of this transformation—or the failure to make it for a persistent minority—are questions of interest to the sociologist and social psychologist. An individual is born with the potentiality for becoming a social being. But whether and how this potentiality is developed and channelled are largely matters of learning. An individual's expectations, attitudes and behavior are developed through contact with adults over a long period of time. His responses to persons and other objects and events in his external environment can be adequately understood only as one understands the traditional meanings which persons, objects and events come to have for him as a result of interacting with those persons who are significant in his experience. The individual never views the external world entirely free from the influence which these culturally defined and socially shared meanings and expectations come to have for him.

The system of traditionally defined meanings, serving as potential guides for behavior and shared with other members of a group, is the phenomenon which we label culture. In becoming a social being, the individual is enculturated or socialized. He learns to play roles appropriate to a wide variety of social situations. When socialized individuals not only share role expectations about behavior but also sanction conformity to these shared expectations, behavior patterns are said to be institutionalized. From this point of view, most drinking behavior can be understood best as an aspect of culture; that is, as shared expectations about behavior. The use or nonuse of alcohol is learned institutionalized behavior for particular groups within the society and integrally related to a number of roles.

The availability of alcohol to members of a society does not in itself explain its use or nonuse as a beverage. Whether one drinks, and what, how, where, when, and with whom one drinks, are institutionalized behavior for particular groups within the society. Although alcohol use is obviously a part of the cultural tradition of the United States, so also is abstinence. And, while drinking is obviously institutionalized for some persons in some groups, whether one is encouraged, permitted or forbidden to drink reflects such social factors as ethnic background, socioeconomic position, religious orientation, age and sex. Some uses of beverage alcohol are institutionalized among Orthodox Jews, for example; and, on the other hand, total abstinence is institutionalized among Mormons. Drinking is generally more permissible for the man than for the woman and for the adult than for the adolescent. Therefore, in being socialized the individual is never exposed to culture in general; he is exposed to particular groups whose members introduce him to the institutionalized roles appropriate for him in that group. The male child, for example, does not learn only how to be a man; he must also learn what it means to be a child as distinct from an adult, or, perhaps, what it means to be a Negro middle-class Presbyterian as distinct from what it means to be a white, lower-class Baptist. He must learn whether or not drinking is ever appropriate; and, if it is, when, where, with whom, and to what extent it is appropriate. An individual's drinking behavior, if he drinks at all, typically conforms to the expectations of significant groups in his social environment.

Adolescence is of particular relevance in understanding the emergence of drinking or abstinent behavior in our society because it is obviously the transition between childhood roles and adult roles. The boundaries of adolescence are not clearly or precisely defined for us. In general terms, introduction to this age-grade comes with puberty, i.e., about age 12 to 15, and is terminated informally by the assumption of adult-like responsibilities, such as marriage, a full-time job or entrance into the armed forces, normally upon graduation from high school at about age 18 or 19, or formally by attaining the age of 21. Adolescence, therefore, is roughly synonymous with the teen years and with participation in the junior and senior high school grades of our educational system. The precise determination of biological ages equivalent to the beginning and end of adolescence is neither possible nor relevant. What is important is the recognition that, in our society, the adolescent is in a transitional period during which he is no longer a child but not yet an adult. Literally the adolescent is in the process of becoming an adult; he is permitted and increasingly required with age to "play at" the institutionalized role behavior associated with adulthood. The adolescent, consequently, learns the attitudes toward and uses of beverage alcohol appropriate to adulthood as he has come to understand what it means to be an adult generally.

Most young people see alcohol integrated into the style of life of many significant adults. This explains, at least in part, why, as one would expect, one finds that among adolescents, the probability of alcohol use—as well as of smoking and some heterosexual activity—and of self-identification as a drinker increases with age, reaching a maximum about the time of graduation from high school. Graduation is the point at which a majority of young people have assumed or will soon assume adult responsibilities associated with a full-time job, marriage or entrance into the armed forces. One or more of these roles is likely to be assumed before the young person has reached the age of 21, the age we usually associate with the end of adolescence.

An adolescent's family and peers are important in the transitional period between childhood and adolescence because he is never introduced to culture in general but rather to the culture as lived by the significant persons in his experience. The significant persons to whom he is most likely to be exposed first, longest and most intimately are adult members of his family. Therefore, what a child comes initially to think about and do with alcohol reflects in large measure what these significant adult role models in his family say about and do with alcohol.

Some of this teaching and learning, although subtle and implicit, nevertheless tends to legitimate the idea of alcohol use: Alcohol is kept in the home without apparent secrecy, shame or guilt and is consumed on a wide variety of occasions without apparent misfortune and with much apparent enjoyment. Some of the teaching is explicit: Occasional experimental "tasting" of alcoholic beverages by children may be tolerated or even encouraged and parents may specify the conditions under which drinking by adolescent members of the family will be permitted. These are probably the experiences of a majority of young people in our society.

A persistent minority of young people, on the other hand, are exposed to a teaching–learning situation in which the significant adult role models to which they are initially exposed are abstinent. In many subtle and obvious ways, a style of life from which alcohol is excluded is transmitted between generations.

This description of how drinking and abstinence as styles of life are transmitted between generations is, of course, overly simple. The process of transmitting family culture to an offspring is complicated by the existence of other agencies of socialization.

The most obvious agency of socialization is the peer group which achieves special significance during adolescent development in our society. The contemporary adolescent occupies an anomalous position in the social structure in that he is no longer a child but not yet an adult. During the relatively long period between puberty and the achievement of adult status, he must orient himself to play at adult roles without, at the same time, being allowed to play them fully. He must learn to behave as adults presumably behave, but at the same time must develop a keen sense of timing and of adult-imposed limitations on his experimentations.

Some observers of the American scene describe adolescence as a time necessarily associated with stress and strain which, in turn, produce a "youth culture" and peer groups antagonistic to adult authority and goals. While this interpretation is certainly plausible, it has not been rigorously tested; the evidence, such as it is, is ambiguous. Some drinking by adolescents undoubtedly reflects hostility toward adult authority and goals. Drinking may be used as a test of loyalty to peer groups precisely because it is discouraged by adults. The contrary evidence, however, is compelling. The probability of alcohol use increases with age, i.e., as the assumption of adult roles is approached. There is a demonstrated relationship between the drinking behavior of parents and their offspring; and given what we know about the importance of parents as models for behavior, a majority of adolescents in our society would in all probability come to use beverage alcohol eventually even if there were no peer group experience at all since young people tend to perceive some drinking as an integral and legitimate part of normal adult behavior. The emphasis of this evidence overwhelmingly favors adolescent identification with adulthood, rather than hostility to adult goals or authority.

While for some young people peer group participation may occasion exposure to models of behavior other than those of the parental family, adolescent cliques tend to form on the basis of similarity of life style developed in the family. And, to the extent to which this is the case, peer group drinking behavior among adolescents would tend to reflect that of the parental models, though perhaps in caricature and to an extent that parents would consider premature and excessive for the adolescent.[3] There is simply no evidence that an abstinent adolescent is inevitably seduced by his peers who drink or that peer group drinking is typically unrestrained by group norms. Research has not clearly identified all the mechanisms which function to keep the nondrinking adolescent the way he is. But the fact remains that a large minority of persons in our society remain abstinent throughout adulthood and that unrestrained drinking is not typical even of organized delinquent gangs.[4] Both nondrinker and drinker can and do find support from peers, but even for the drinker this support is ordinarily conditional. The myth of inevitable and irresistible peer group pressure to drink and to drink excessively may tend to become, unfortunately, a kind of self-fulfilling prophecy.

The proposition that young people do not invent ideas of drinking or abstinence but learn them in the process of being socialized as adults is supported by the evidence of this study. Before this evidence is presented, however, it is appropriate to review the growing body of literature which describes and interprets what various persons in our society do with and think about alcohol. Alcohol use in our society is more heavily freighted than most other behavior with conflicting emotions and moral evaluations. Consequently, social science studies of drinking behavior which focus on description and interpretation as distinct from evaluation of the rightness and wrongness of this behavior are few and recent. Why this is so is suggested in the following chapter. This next chapter will also review selected investigations of drinking behavior which provide the background for a sociological and social psychological study of drinking among teen-agers.

[3] See, for example, the discussion of peer group accentuation of parental behavior in Gusfield (30).

[4] On this point see Cloward and Ohlin (12).

Chapter 2

DRINKING IS SOCIAL BEHAVIOR

THE USE OF ALCOHOL as a beverage is part of our complex heritage and has been since Colonial times. Most adults in our society now use, and apparently for a number of generations have used, beverage alcohol at least sometimes. For most of them, drinking is and remains an integral part of a style of life, a way of relating themselves to the environment. They learned this pattern of behavior from their parents and peers and they will transmit it in many ways, both subtle and direct, to their children. Drinking is ordinarily one among many aspects of their experience, not the pivot around which life revolves. Persons who drink are aware that alcohol can do something to them as well as for them, but the possible disadvantages of use apparently are more often than not balanced by the rewards associated with drinking.

For a persistent minority drinking does get out of hand, and does involve them in irresponsible behavior that is costly, both personally and socially. Sometimes alcohol does become the pivot around which life revolves. Such drinkers are a troublesome and highly visible minority. Describing and interpreting the behavior of the drinkers who are problems and create problems has, until quite recently, been the major research interest of those interested in alcohol use, to the neglect, almost to the exclusion, of research on the drinking behavior characteristic of the majority of users.

The "Social Problem" Orientation to Drinking

A primary reason why research attention has typically been directed to the pathological aspects of alcohol use is that all drinking has frequently been conceived as abnormal, as maladaptive, or as only a prelude to alcoholism. From this point of view, the distinction between drinking, drunkenness and alcoholism has often been reduced to one of degree and duration. This focus on the most visible and dramatic aspects of alcohol use has placed a decisive stamp on orientations to the study of drinking, on the formulation of research questions, and on the types of explanations of drinking behavior which have been proposed. The personal and social dysfunctions of drinking have been emphasized almost to the exclusion of any broader consideration of drinking as an acceptable form of social behavior.

The tendency of many Americans in their public discussions to equate all drinking with abnormality and all inebriety with alcoholism derives in part from a dual tradition about the use of alcohol which is an integral part of the American cultural heritage. On the one hand, there is the tradition of "the Protestant Ethic," to use Weber's well known phrase. About this ethic[1] Edwin M. Lemert says:

> "It is entirely possible that persons strongly indoctrinated with the Anglo-Saxon, middle-class drinking ethic, or perhaps with that which is called the 'Protestant Ethic,' symbolize drinking in this kind of context as evidence of loss of control over the self, which is a cardinal sin in the Protestant middle-class value system. Each drink is a symbolic 'giving in' to a hated impulse; failures and inadequacies of all sorts become symbolized as consequences of a basic character weakness, centering around and corroborating an internal picture of the self as a sot and a drunkard, which must be erased or escaped by further intoxication. Each return to sobriety etches the self picture in sharper relief and renews the stimulus to drink" (49, *p. 366*).

The tradition of temperance—interestingly defined as total abstinence by the temperance movement in the United States—has concentrated attention on the presumed immorality of all drinking. On the other hand, as observers of the American scene have noted, most adults and older adolescents drink at some time and this drinking at least gives the appearance of being approved and prudently provided for by themselves and their peers (17, 55, 56, 71, 82).

The personal and social costs associated with inebriety and alcoholism in our society are impressive and cannot be ignored. The estimated 4 to 5 million alcoholics in the United States, for example, clearly constitute a major health problem.[2] Moreover, in a highly complex, mechanized society, the depressant effect of alcohol on human response mechanisms has serious implications for safety and for personal and social responsibility. These im-

[1] See also Warner, McPeek and Jellinek (88).

[2] There were an estimated 4½ million alcoholics in the United States in 1960, constituting a rate of approximately 4 alcoholics for every 100 adults in the population (44). Alcoholics are defined as those who manifest "repeated implicative drinking so as to cause injury to the drinker's health or to his social or economic functioning."

plications are reflected in part by statistics indicating that the number of automobile and industrial accidents directly or indirectly attributable to drinking may be high. Although these practical problems of health, safety and responsibility can only speculatively be converted into dollars and cents, the economic cost is estimated to be high.[8]

The orientation to alcohol in terms of the problems its use creates has drawn attention to the urgency of "doing something" about it. But the attempt to identify what this "something" should be has not always been associated with increased understanding of why drinking persists in spite of its potential detrimental consequences. Pleas for total abstinence on moral grounds or for legal prohibition imply that the reason for drinking is to be found in the alcohol itself, and that once drinking stopped the various problems associated with it would disappear. From this point of view, the emphasis tends always to be on the effects of drinking rather than on its causes. The initial focus of scientific research on the physiological and psychological consequences of drinking frequently and in large quantities supported, though in large part unintentionally, this orientation to drinking behavior in terms of what alcohol does to the drinker.

Understanding the physiological effects of alcohol is of course important. A growing body of scientific literature appropriately deals with these questions. Alcohol has been found to be an anesthetic with decided depressant effects on the physiological and psychological functions of the human body. Excessive drinking over long periods of time jeopardizes health. No convincing evidence has revealed, however, that the initial or continued use of alcohol can be explained in physiological and pharmacological terms alone. Yet there has been a persistent popular tendency to explain alcoholism, and by implication all drinking, in terms of the properties of alcohol and its effects on the human organism alone.

Psychiatrists and clinical psychologists have also tended to be preoccupied with the abnormal use of alcohol. Their focus has been characteristically on disturbed personalities or on the personality disturbances apparently resulting from or associated with extreme

[8] For an assessment which estimates that the direct economic costs of hospitalization, wage loss and property loss attributable to intoxication and alcoholism alone were in excess of three-quarters of a billion dollars a year in the 1940's, see Landis (47).

use. "Anxiety reduction," "reduction of superego demands," "regression," "latent homosexuality," "negation," and similar phrases fill the pages of this literature.[4] While there is, of course, no objection to charting the personality dynamics involved in certain types of drinking, nor to specifying the pharmacological and physiological aspects of the use of alcohol, by focusing on extreme use by a minority of drinkers the social aspects of drinking have been minimized. Psychiatric and psychological research, for example, have not ordinarily been concerned with questions about why alcohol rather than some other depressant is used by some disturbed people, why most drinkers have no problems with alcohol, or why all disturbed people or even all "excessive drinkers" are not also alcoholics. Psychological and psychiatric research on drinking, characteristically preoccupied with the intrapsychic processes of abnormal drinkers, discouraged the investigation of sociocultural factors in the etiology of abnormal drinking behavior and of the uses of alcohol that remained within the normal range. Exceptions can be found, but they are rare (65, 87).

In the past two decades two important new emphases have appeared in research on alcohol use. First, there has been a growing consensus that the origins of drinking behavior, including the abnormal variety, cannot be accounted for in terms of physiological processes and individual psychology; social and cultural factors are also important in understanding the use or avoidance of alcohol. Recognition that sociocultural factors contribute to abnormal drinking behavior does not mean that the other perspectives are irrelevant or unimportant. It does mean that drinking behavior cannot be adequately understood in terms of a single point of view, especially a point of view that concentrates only on the individual organism or psyche. Second, there has been a growing consensus among researchers interested in alcohol studies that more attention should be given to understanding drinking behavior in general and not just its extreme forms. The breadth of these recent emphases is reflected, for example, in the observation of one prominent student of drinking behavior:

"The use of alcoholic beverages by [the members of] society has primarily a symbolic meaning, and secondarily it achieves 'function.' Cultures which accept this custom differ in the nature and degree of

[4] For example, see Fleeson and Gildea (25), Schilder (74) and Strecker (83). For a comprehensive survey of this literature, see Jellinek (41, *pp. 55 ff.*).

the 'functions' which they regard as legitimate. The differences in these 'functions' are determined by the general pattern of the culture, e.g., the need for the release and for special control of aggression, the need and the ways and means of achieving identification, the nature and intensity of anxieties and the modus of their relief and so forth. The more the symbolic character of the custom is preserved, the less room will be granted by the culture to the 'functions' of drinking.

"Any drinking within the accepted ways is symptomatic of the culture of which the drinker is a member. Within that frame of cultural symptomatology there may be in addition individual symptoms expressed in the act of drinking. The fact that a given individual drinks a glass of beer with his meal may be the symptom of the culture which accepts such use as a refreshment, or as a 'nutritional supplement.' That this individual drinks at this given moment may be a symptom of his fatigue, or his elation or some other mood and thus an individual symptom, but if his culture accepts the use for these purposes it is at the same time a cultural symptom.

"In this sense even the small or moderate use of alcoholic beverages is symptomatic, and it may be said that all drinkers are culturally symptomatic drinkers or, at least, started as such.

"The vast majority of the users of alcoholic beverages stay within the limits of the culturally accepted drinking behaviors and drink predominantly as an expression of their culture and, while individual expression may be present in these behaviors its role remains insignificant" (40).[5]

The ideas presented in this passage constitute a fundamental reorientation to the study and understanding of drinking behavior. This orientation clearly shifts the emphasis from the individual viewed in isolation to individuals placed in the sociocultural contexts in which they operate. Attention is shifted from the compulsive drinking of the alcoholic to the more basic consideration of the significance of drinking as one type of social behavior. If the cited passage reflected only the considered judgment of a single person, it would, perhaps, be interesting but of limited significance. However, in a way this passage summarizes concisely the trend evident in two decades of research on the uses of beverage alcohol, stimulated in large part by the Yale (now Rutgers) Center of Alcohol Studies.

From its foundation in 1940 the Yale (now Rutgers) Center of Alcohol Studies has emphasized the research utility of approaching drinking as behavior which must be studied within the framework

[5] This point of view is comparable to that developed by Lindesmith (50) with regard to the symbolic aspects of the use of opiates; though Lindesmith specifically excludes a consideration of alcoholism in his study, he does suggest the possible social psychological similarities between the use of opiates and some uses of alcohol.

of many disciplines simultaneously. The initial problem of the Center was to accumulate and systematize existing evidence from relevant disciplines and to guide future research in terms of filling gaps in the understanding of drinking behavior. One of the most obvious gaps was information about *normal* uses of alcohol. The need was recognized, and articulated particularly by the sociologist Selden D. Bacon, for sociological and anthropological studies concentrating on representative samples of the drinking population rather than on the clinical study of a minority of abnormal drinkers. In Bacon's words, "Until the drinking behavior of a representative sample of the drinking population [in a society] is observed, described, and analyzed, characterization of a portion [of that population] as abnormal is likely to reflect fallacy and bias" (2). A long range program designed to summarize existing sociological and anthropological data and to coordinate continued research in these areas was proposed as early as 1944.

This proposed program of the Center of Alcohol Studies has matured in two directions of interest here. The first has been the accumulation of comparative data on the drinking behavior of peoples around the world. This research, done primarily by anthropologists, has emphasized the diversity of drinking behavior among the peoples of the world. The second direction has been toward the accumulation of data about drinking behavior in the United States. This research, done primarily by sociologists, has been confined largely to surveys from which descriptive statistical summaries of drinking behavior have been compiled.[6]

There are several reasons for reporting here brief summaries of some of the more important of these studies which concentrate on drinking behavior rather than on alcoholism per se. First, until the present time the findings of social science studies in this area have not been systematically surveyed.[7] Second, these studies provide a relevant background for our study of teen-age drinking. Attention, therefore, will be directed first to brief summaries of selected anthropological studies of drinking and then to a summary of survey data on drinking in the United States.

[6] The QUARTERLY JOURNAL OF STUDIES ON ALCOHOL and its cumulative *Classified Abstract Archive of the Alcohol Literature* are the best sources of published sociological and anthropological research on drinking.

[7] Attention has recently been given to summarizing anthropological research on alcohol use by Washburne (90).

Anthropological Studies of Drinking Behavior

One of the early studies directed specifically to an analysis of drinking behavior in relation to culture is Ruth Bunzel's comparative analysis of the use of alcohol by Indians in a Mexican and a Guatemalan village (9). She notes that, in spite of the fact that the Mexican Chamula were known as "bad Indians," there was a striking absence of aggressive behavior accompanying heavy drinking, even though social penalties for such aggression were light. Aggression, such as it was, was largely verbal and physical encounters were limited entirely to the use of the hands. Weapons were never used even in drunken brawls.[8] Alcohol use among these Indians appears to be a focal point around which many social activities, particularly convivial interaction, take place. Drunkenness is expected and taken as a matter of course.

This description of the Mexican Chamula is in sharp contrast to Bunzel's description of the Guatemalan Indian whose Mayan cultural heritage predisposes him to a morality which values abstinence. Secular drinking is a modern phenomenon among Mayan Indians, confined primarily to fiestas, and accompanied by increased eroticism followed by guilt feelings. The sense of guilt apparently stems from the sexual promiscuity associated with drinking and not the act of drinking.[9] Bunzel concludes from her comparative study that drinking is qualitatively a very different phenomenon in these two cultures and that in each case the differences must be understood in cultural terms.

The research of Donald Horton (38) provides a comprehensive ethnological survey of drinking behavior in 56 societies selected from the Human Relations Area Files. Horton presents "a theory of psychological and social functions" as an explanation of certain aspects of the drinking customs of primitive peoples. His study is organized around the proposition that "the primary function of the

[8] A similar observation has been made on the behavior of the Mixe Indians by Beale (5). The Mixe are reported to quarrel frequently, especially when drunk. Although weapons are always carried, when quarreling begins, participants who have been drinking hand over their weapons to bystanders. Similarly, in the Mohave society, Devereux (16) notes the use of alcohol as a mechanism for aggression avoidance. The Mohave man is capable of "passing out" after a single drink of alcohol when aggressive behavior is directed toward him by others.

[9] This is in contrast to observations made about the guilt feelings said to accompany drinking among persons in the western world who subscribe to the "Protestant ethic." On this point see the passage from Lemert quoted above.

consumption of alcohol in any society is more adequately explained by its anxiety-reducing function than any other function." Having specified that drinking is a learned mechanism of anxiety-reduction, Horton investigated the relationship between situations which are expected to be anxiety-producing (e.g., famine, disease, war and the threat of war) and degrees of inebriety and reports a positive relationship. He also reports a positive relationship between inebriety and releases of physical aggression, including sexual aggression.

Equally important in this study is the documentation of the variation in cultural definitions and social structure which affect drinking behavior. Horton notes, for example, that the response of a people to "anxiety-producing" situations is not invariably inebriety. Stringent social controls are typically found to accompany the use of alcohol in the presence of "real" imminent danger. Moreover, in various societies differences in drinking behavior are observed on the basis of age, sex and other status factors. Drinking is found to be almost exclusively group behavior and alcohol is found on occasion to provide one basis for the symbolic identification of an in-group. In brief, Horton's findings suggest that drinking, even drinking that results in inebriety, is culturally defined and socially structured behavior.

Robert Freed Bales (4) continued Horton's and Bunzel's emphasis on the sociocultural aspects of drinking behavior with a study of two identifiable ethnic sub-groups in American society, the Irish and the Jews. Bales observes that, while the incidence of drinking is high in both groups, the rates of alcoholism are strikingly different. The Jewish alcoholic is rare in contrast to the high incidence of alcoholism reported among the Irish. Bales observed differences in alcoholism rates in terms of three variables (*1*) the ways in which culture operates in a particular context to bring about social disequilibrium and personal anxieties; (*2*) the kinds of attitudes which are shared by individuals in a society toward the use of alcohol; and (*3*) the extent to which suitable alternative mechanisms of adjustment are provided. Like Horton, Bales chooses to emphasize the anxiety-reducing functions of drinking, particularly in regard to the excesses of the abnormal drinker. At the same time Bales notes that, even in the absence of extreme anxiety, alcohol may play an integral part in social interaction. As Bunzel concluded about the Chamula, Bales concludes that individuals may drink because it is an integral part of a way of life or because they enjoy it and not only in those situations which provoke anxiety. People may be variously predisposed to use alcohol ritually (as in Communion), convivially (as at a party), or instrumentally (as when a salesman buys drinks for prospective customers), as well as to reduce anxiety. The use of alcohol thus has no necessary meaning and no universal function; it may have a variety of meanings and functions.[10] Moreover, Bales stresses that there may be alternative mechanisms which "do for" individuals and groups what alcohol presumably does. Among these alternatives may be listed the strong tea and coffee of the Moslem, the ecstasy of the Balinese, the ritual of the totally abstinent Zuñi or the opiates of the Oriental.[11]

What drinking means, then, and what alcohol is expected to do for as well as to the drinker are significantly structured and regulated by cultural definition. Drinking must be understood in the context of a way of life. J. J. Honigmann and I. Honigmann (37) have further documented this point in a study of drinking in a small community along the Alaskan highway populated by Canadian whites and Athabaskan-speaking Indians. Alcohol was found in this community to be a symbolic means for bridging the social distance between individuals and groups. Heightened sexual aggressiveness did not typically accompany drinking in either group, but drinking was used as a means of symbolic aggression on the part of both whites and Indians against stringent legal controls imposed by the provincial government on the purchase of alcohol. Different styles of drinking were apparent, however. Whites characteristically "sipped and relished" whisky and their drinking was accompanied by clowning. Indians tended to gulp their liquor and clowning was absent. Drinking was largely confined in both groups to social activities and rarely interfered with their work habits.

Finally, special attention is deserved by a study (49) of uses of beverage alcohol by Northwest Coast Indians, including the Salish,

[10] For other studies of the relationship between different culturally defined meanings of drinking and differential functions of the use of alcohol see Glad (27), Landman (48), Lolli et al. (53) and Snyder (79).

[11] With regard to the Chinese and Japanese, LaBarre (46) observes that these people use alcoholic beverages without the slightest trace of the ambivalence frequently noted in the western world. The solitary drinker is unthinkable. There is no violent addiction and alcoholic frenzy is rare. Intoxication has little moral significance and the primary control of drinking comes through the positive emphasis on the honoring of social obligations. See on this point also Benedict (7).

Nootka, Kwakiutl, Tsimshian and Haida. In this account Lemert reports the patterns of drinking behavior observable among these Indians in relation to status, roles, symbolic values, verbalized purposes and emotional qualities. Of particular interest were the public and self-image of the drinker. In brief, Lemert is concerned with an exploration of the meaning, symbolic associations, and sentiments attached to drinking by individuals as members of social groups.

Lemert made his study at a time when the traditional Indian way of life on the Northwest Coast was in a state of disintegration. Acculturation through contact with whites was well advanced and drinking had acquired symbolic significance as a mechanism of aggression, primarily against the white man and his laws. The Indians did not associate drinking with sexual aggression; among the whites, however, inebriety seemed to be a means particularly adapted to the seduction of the Indian woman. Apart from the symbolic aggression against the whites, drinking among the Indians was generally associated with convivial and traditional ritualistic behavior.

The Indian's drinking was also clearly related to social status and his conception of his status. By histrionic drinking he could in effect say, "Look, this is the way I drink," and in this act express his conception of what it means to be a man or to be a man of high status. By means of drinking the Indian could also assert his equality with the whites and at the same time perpetuate the old rivalry patterns of competition in wealth and display which have been traditional among the Northwest Coast Indians. This is illustrated particularly in the case of the drinking feast.

The drinking feasts of the Northwest Coast Indians were more than occasions to display status as the potlatch, after which the feasts were patterned, had been. The drinking party was an occasion for challenges and displays of status symbols, one of which was a large supply of illegal alcohol. Moreover, this party was an occasion for satirical songs and for the free expression of feelings and impulses. Horseplay, verbal aggression and personal debunking directed toward persons of high status were forms of aggression largely occasioned by and confined to drinking situations and were tolerated only in such drinking situations.

The Northwest Coast Indians had permissive attitudes toward drinking and drunkenness. The most common reaction of a sober person to an inebriate was of caution and avoidance. Concepts of blame and sin were not associated with drinking; on the contrary, a positive feeling of gain in breaking the law of the white man, who prohibited sale of alcohol to Indians, was recognized.

From his data, Lemert concludes that group demands on behavior are integral to understanding the drinking of these Indians. So long as an Indian remained an Indian, he had certain obligations to express himself in interaction with others and had to do so by means of the instruments at hand. The use of alcohol cannot be explained, therefore, in the essentially negative terms of anxiety-reduction alone. Alcohol may do something for the individual in relationship to the group and for a group in relation to other groups. The notion that alcohol can only do something to and not for individuals and groups or that social integration cannot be based in any way on the use of alcohol reflects the moralistic cultural bias of the "Protestant Ethic" rather than objective analysis. Alcohol and its use, like other objects and forms of behavior, may be used to support the important values of a society even when drinking is not in itself positively valued.

In summary, the anthropological studies briefly surveyed stress the importance of viewing the use of beverage alcohol as culturally defined and socially structured behavior. Drinking behavior in a particular society is viewed most adequately within the context of a way of life. Though certain concentrations of ingested alcohol have consistent physiological effects on the human organism, the effects of drinking on behavior vary in important aspects from society to society. For example, the use of alcohol may, but does not necessarily, result in heightened aggression and sexuality. Drinking, even when "excessive," is typically social behavior subject to group control. Who will drink what, when, where and with whom are rarely, if ever, matters of chance alone. Moreover, drinking which results repeatedly in getting drunk does not necessarily result in alcoholism, and the association of sin and guilt with all drinking is apparently confined largely to segments of modern western society. Rates of alcohol consumption and the incidence of alcoholism are not at all positively correlated in every society.[12]

[12] For an elaboration of these points, with particular reference to differences in drinking behavior and attitudes toward drinking in various countries of western Europe, see Jellinek (41, *Ch. 2*).

Surveys of Drinking Behavior in the United States

Studies of drinking behavior in the United States have been limited primarily to descriptive surveys.[13] These surveys do, however, provide basic information about the extent and pattern of the use of alcohol in our society, some of the significant characteristics of drinkers, and the social situations which are most likely to be associated with drinking. Therefore, brief summaries of several of these studies will be presented in the following paragraphs. The differences in drinking behavior as they are related to age and sex in the United States are of special relevance to the findings discussed in subsequent chapters.

In 1946 the National Opinion Research Center conducted a nationwide survey of drinking behavior among persons aged 21 and over (71, 72). In the representative national sample polled, 65% of the respondents reported themselves to be drinkers (not abstinent) and 17% of these drinkers identified themselves as "regular" drinkers (more than three times a week). Men were more likely than women to be drinkers (75% as compared to 56%) and more likely to be "regular" drinkers (27% as compared to 7%). Those living in urban areas were also more likely to be drinkers than those in rural areas (77% as compared to 46%).[14]

Attention shifted from the whole adult population to the late adolescent and young adult in college when Straus and Bacon (82) administered questionnaires to 17,000 students in 27 colleges selected to represent different types of financing, enrollment and regions of the United States during 1950 and 1951. Although 74% of the students in this survey reported themselves to be "users" (that is, alcohol use not confined solely to an isolated experience or religious ritual), the proportion varied in the various colleges from 92% to 65% among men and 89% to 39% among women. Among these college students, the users were more likely to come from higher income families than were the abstainers. Religious affiliation was also found to be associated with drinking. Jews and Catholics were more likely to drink than were Protestants; Mormons were the

[13] Comparative studies of ethnic subgroups which have already been noted are an exception; other exceptions include Bacon (1), Macrory (56) and Dollard (17).

[14] These national data are supported by research in the state of Washington reported by Maxwell (58). On the basis of polling a random sample, Maxwell reports that 63% of the adult population reported themselves as drinkers. Men were more likely than women to be drinkers (76% compared to 51%) and more likely to be "regular" drinkers (19% compared to 3%).

least likely of any religious group to drink. With the exception of Mormons, however, college students of all religious affiliations were more likely to be users than abstainers.

Age and sex were found to be related to drinking among these college students. Users tended to increase with age, reaching a high proportion at about the age of 21 and diminishing slightly after that. Women were more likely than men to report themselves as abstinent.

The morality of drinking typically was qualified situationally. Both men and women applied a dual standard to the appropriateness of men and women drinking. There was general agreement that drinking is more appropriate for men than for women and also more appropriate for adults than for nonadults. Abstainers, however, did not characteristically generalize their abstinence as morally "right" for all other college students.

Most student drinkers reported that they had learned to drink prior to entering college. Parental approval of their behavior was generally claimed by drinkers; 43% of them indicated that they had had experience with alcohol before reaching puberty.

Recognition that drinking is learned behavior which is culturally defined and socially structured, and apparently well developed by late adolescence, has focused attention increasingly on adolescence. This is the case because it is during adolescence that, for a majority of persons in our society, the abstinence of childhood is transformed more often than not into the drinking behavior characteristic of adulthood. To date, however, research on what adolescents think about and do with beverage alcohol has been confined to descriptive surveys. Moreover, attention has been focused almost exclusively on the teen-age adolescents in high school.[15]

The first of these studies (54) of the teen-ager was conducted in a suburban high school in Washington, D. C., in 1941 with replications in 1945 and 1947. Here, in contrast to the studies of the adult and of the late adolescent in college, the large majority of high-school teen-agers reported themselves as nondrinkers (abstainers). Although the percentage of abstainers decreased in each restudy, in 1947 only 45% of the boys and 23% of the girls reported themselves as drinkers.

A study (77) of drinking by adolescents was also conducted in

[15] Several studies of drinking among preadolescents have been reported, but these have concentrated on specific ethnic subgroups; see Footnote 10, supra.

the state of Utah among over 1,000 tenth and twelfth grade students attending selected public high schools. The schools were chosen on the basis of size and location in the state. Forty-four per cent of the boys and 21% of the girls reported themselves as drinkers. Although an overwhelming majority of students in this study "disapproved" of teen-agers drinking, the number of disapprovers tended to decrease with rising age. When drinking among adolescents occurs, it was thought by these high-school students most likely to occur first in the home. Among the most common reasons given by them for drinking among their peers were "to be with the crowd" and "to be gay."

A third study (34) was made in Nassau County, New York, among 1,000 high-school students. While 86% of these students indicated they were not abstinent, only 43% reported having used alcohol during the previous week, suggesting the need for caution in interpreting such data. A person who identifies himself as "not abstinent" clearly is not necessarily a "regular drinker."

Ninety-three per cent of the Nassau County students reported that their parents drank and a majority indicated that they had drunk at home with parental approval. The percentage of students drinking was found to increase with age but to reach a plateau at about age 19. The most frequently designated occasions for drinking were at parties, celebrations and special events.

Two other surveys of drinking behavior and attitudes toward alcohol use among teen-agers in high school, one in Wisconsin (95) and another in Kansas (43), have used the questionnaire and procedure of the Nassau County survey. Apart from pointing up regional variations, the findings of all three surveys are quite similar.[16]

The survey findings reported here suggest that, contrary to expectations fostered by concentration on the abnormal or problem drinker, drinking behavior which cannot be easily classified as abnormal appears to be characteristic of a majority of the adult population in the United States. Moreover, this "normal" drinking is not observed randomly in the population. Differences in both the frequency and the patterns of drinking are related to age, sex and religious affiliation, to mention only three factors. The data indicate further both that basic orientations to drinking appear to be

[16] For a detailed comparison of the findings of these and the other studies of drinking among teen-agers in high school, see Maddox (57).

learned in the context of the home and peer group associations and that experimentation with or exposure to drinking typically begins during adolescence or before. Moreover, cultural definitions of the appropriateness of drinking make this behavior less appropriate for adolescents than for adults and less appropriate for women than for men. Though appropriateness also has a moral dimension—the "rightness" or "wrongness" of drinking—the findings do not indicate either that the majority of "normal" drinkers consider their behavior immoral or that all abstainers necessarily consider drinking by others to be immoral. There is also the suggestion that alcohol is defined as a social beverage rather than as a drug, since the most common situations associated with drinking are social and convivial. The party, the ceremony, the special event appear to be the situations most likely to suggest drinking.

SUMMARY

An emergent interest in understanding drinking behavior in general, and not just "abnormal" drinking behavior has appeared in social science research during the past two decades. The study of drinking behavior, which in the United States has been focused on alcoholism, giving a distinctive stamp to the formulation of research problems, has been broadened. In the past, primary attention has been devoted to what "excessive" use of alcohol does to the individual and subsequently to society. Research has been primarily physiological and psychological and has concentrated on the individual. The physiological and psychological aspects of drinking, while important to any comprehensive understanding of drinking behavior, have nevertheless provided an incomplete understanding of this behavior. Increasing interest has been shown in the learned social aspects of drinking behavior as indicated by an increasing number of anthropological and sociological studies which approach drinking as culturally defined and socially structured behavior.

Anthropological research has established several general propositions which may be taken as basic for subsequent research:

1. Uses of beverage alcohol and the "effects" on behavior vary from one society to another. This does not mean that the physiological effects of the same amounts of alcohol for comparable individuals are necessarily different; rather the social expectations are

different. Alcoholism, intoxication and drinking are not identical forms of behavior.

2. Drinking may do something for as well as to individuals and the groups in which they interact. Alcohol use may be positively valued behavior which contributes directly or indirectly to the achievement of desired personal and social goals.

3. Drinking characteristically is social behavior subject to group controls. The idea of alcohol use is not invented; it is learned. Shared rules specifying who drinks what, where, when, how and with whom are also learned. While the drinking of some violates the expectations of their peers, this is not the case for the majority of drinkers in any society.

Surveys concentrating on the pattern and social context of drinking illustrate the above points and also establish several additional points about the use of alcohol in the United States which provide a background for subsequent research:

1. Drinking is common adult behavior, not universally accompanied by ambivalence, shame or fear.

2. Drinking is social behavior typically subject to group controls. Drinking is learned. Like those in other societies, Americans also learn shared rules specifying who drinks what, where, when, how and with whom. Age and sex distinctions appear to be especially relevant in understanding differences in drinking behavior in our society.

3. Drinking may do something for as well as to individuals and the groups in which they participate. Although the institutionalized aspects of drinking have not been studied extensively in our society, the groundwork for such study has been laid.

These social science studies of alcohol use provide the background of the study which is reported in the following chapters. Attention will be given in the next chapter to describing and interpreting patterns of alcohol use and abstinence among selected teenagers in high school.

Chapter 3

PATTERNS OF DRINKING AND ABSTINENCE

THE PRINCIPAL CONCERN of this chapter is to describe patterns of drinking behavior and abstinence among eleventh and twelfth grade students in the high schools of a midwestern city. *Pattern of drinking behavior* as it is used here refers to events and circumstances which are regularly associated with the act of drinking, including the specific uses of alcohol as they occur in time and space, whether and how the use of alcohol is considered a part of the self-image of the user, and the location of users within one or another social group.[1] Consideration is given, correspondingly, to the *pattern of abstinence.*

In the chapters that follow a teen-ager is considered to be a *user* of alcohol if he reports that his exposure to alcohol has not been confined to isolated tastes or drinks but is recurrent, however infrequent this may be. The student who reports no recurrent use of beverage alcohol is designated a *nonuser.*

The students were also asked whether they preferred to think of themselves and to be thought of as *drinkers* or *nondrinkers.* This question was designed to explore the relationship between the use of alcohol and the inclusion of this act as part of the self-image of the user. Everyone develops through time a portrait of himself, a perception of his own person both as a discrete entity and as one who stands in relation to other persons or selves.[2] For the adolescent the development of a sense of individual identity is a crucial problem. Erik H. Erikson (22, 23, 24) considers this the crucial problem of the adolescent who is building a bridge between what he was as a child and what he is about to be as an adult. Whether or not the young people in this study preferred to think of themselves or be thought of as drinkers or as nondrinkers is not considered *the* crucial piece of information which totally defines their emerging conception of self or sense of personal identity. Their choice in this regard is considered an important piece of information about how they relate themselves to a commonly used social object, alcohol, and a commonly observed social act among adults, drinking.

[1] For additional comments on the concept of pattern of drinking see Lemert (49).
[2] On the concept of self see Cohen (13, *pp. 189 ff.*) and Goffman (28).

In the analysis which follows, attention is given to the matter of self-identification with alcohol use as something to be explained, just as the act of using or not using alcohol is to be explained.

In the chapters that follow then, *users* will sometimes be subdivided into those who designated themselves as *drinkers* and those who designated themselves as *nondrinkers*. The *nonusers* constitute the third major category among the adolescents in this study. After a description of the various responses to alcohol by these selected teen-agers, they will be located within the community in which they live by patterns of use or abstinence.

A Description of Responses to Alcohol

Prevalence of Drinking and Drinkers

Determination of the prevalence of teen-age drinking must be distinguished from determination of the prevalence of self-designated drinkers. When the 1,962 high-school students in the study (903 boys and 1,059 girls) were asked, "Do you consider yourself to be a drinker?" only 177 (about 9%), of whom 48 were girls, responded affirmatively. All of these students were found to be actually users. An additional 279 (14.2%) students, of whom 107 were girls, designated themselves nondrinkers but reported recurrent use of alcohol. Thus, 456 (23.2%) of the students in the study were found to be users: 301 boys and 155 girls.

Among the nonusers 13% of the boys and 15% of the girls reported that they had never tasted alcohol. At the other extreme, 13.6% of the 177 drinkers and only 2 nondrinkers reported that they drink "often" or "very often." Students who reported extensive drinking, therefore, constitute only slightly more than 1% of all the teen-agers studied and about 6% of the users.

Depending on the criteria chosen, the prevalence of drinking and self-designated drinkers among these students may be described in several different ways:

(*1*) 92% of the teen-agers studied had drunk or tasted alcohol at some time;

(*2*) 23% reported that they are not abstainers and that they drink some alcoholic beverage at least occasionally;

(*3*) 9% designated themselves as drinkers;

(*4*) 8% indicated that they had never tasted alcohol;

(5) about 6% of the users reported frequent consumption of alcohol.

The possible significance of this reluctance of some users to designate themselves as drinkers in spite of the fact that they reported drinking on some occasions is suggested in the interview data. The students made definite distinctions between "tasters," "social drinkers," and the "drinker–drunkard–alcoholic." One student described succinctly the frequently encountered objection to the designation of oneself as a "drinker":

"If you asked me if I were a drinker, I would think you were asking me if I go out every night and I'd tell you no, because I don't drink often. But if you ask me if I drink rarely, I'd say yes, because I do. I consider myself a person who drinks but not a drinker."

"Social drinking" for these teen-agers implies "going out on the town, all fixed up and maybe talking to someone," or "being with the crowd." As for distinctions among drinkers, drunkards, and alcoholics, there was less clarity although they were clearly distinguishable from social drinkers. The drinker–drunkard was typically described as a person "who spends most of his time drinking." Emphasis was placed on the extent of, motivation for, and degree of dependence on drinking, although none of these points was developed by students with much precision. Major emphasis was placed by them on distinguishing the drinker–drunkard–alcoholic from the social drinker. While the former was sometimes described as a person "drowning his sorrow" with alcohol or one who "just can't stay away from it," the latter was never referred to in these terms. This suggests that for the self-designated drinker this label was the equivalent of social drinker. The drinking self-designated nondrinker, on the other hand, appears to have attached a different and unacceptable meaning to the same label.

At least two other explanations of the reluctance of some users to identify themselves as drinkers may be suggested here in anticipation of subsequent discussion. The drinking nondrinker may reflect the adolescent who is experimenting with the use of alcohol but has not yet integrated its use with his conception of self. Or, this apparently contradictory behavior may reflect ambivalence on the part of some adolescents who drink but find this behavior morally unacceptable. More will be said about this later.

What and How Much do Teen-Age Students Drink?

Beer is the most frequently used beverage of boy users (Table 1).[3] Slightly more than half report drinking one or more bottles of beer

TABLE 1.—*Estimates of Personal Consumption of Beer, Wine, Whisky and Mixed Drinks in an Average Week among Users, By Sex and Self-Designation, in Per Cent*

	Nondrinkers		Drinkers	
Average weekly consumption	*Boys*	*Girls*	*Boys*	*Girls*
Beer				
Rarely or never use	89	94	44	73
Between 1 and 3 bottles	5	6	22	15
Between 3 and 6 bottles	5	0	19	8
More than 6 bottles	1	0	13	2
No answer*	0	0	2	2
Totals	*100*	*100*	*100*	*100*
Wine				
Rarely or never use	82	91	60	61
Between 1 and 3 wine glasses	8	5	18	25
Between 3 and 6 wine glasses	0	0	5	0
More than 6 wine glasses	2	0	3	4
No answer*	8	4	14	10
Totals	*100*	*100*	*100*	*100*
Whisky				
Rarely or never use	86	90	64	69
Between 1 and 3 shot glasses	4	3	16	17
Between 3 and 6 shot glasses	2	1	5	4
More than 6 shot glasses	†	0	6	2
No answer*	8	6	9	8
Totals	*100*	*100*	*100*	*100*
Mixed Drinks				
Rarely or never use	79	84	63	69
Between 1 and 3 mixed drinks	7	8	9	19
Between 3 and 6 mixed drinks	2	0	4	2
More than 6 mixed drinks	0	0	3	2
No answer*	12	8	21	8
Totals	*100*	*100*	*100*	*100*
N	172	107	129	48

* "No answer" is probably most adequately interpreted as "never use."
† Less than 1%.

[3] The credibility of reported amounts and frequency of drinking was not investigated. Both the tests of reliability of the questionnaire and impressions from interviews with students provide a basis for confidence in the consistency of responses. Subsequently, however, it should be understood that references to student behavior refer to reported behavior, not observed or confirmed behavior.

in an average week and one in eight of them reported drinking six or more bottles. Although one in four of the girl drinkers indicates the consumption of one or more bottles of beer during an average week, the reported amount of their drinking is much less than that indicated by the boys.

The self-designated nondrinkers among the users did not report using any alcoholic beverage very frequently and no particular beverage was singled out by them. Eleven per cent of the boys and 6% of the girls in this category reported drinking at least one bottle of beer in the average week. Wine, the second most frequently reported beverage of drinkers, is used by approximately the same percentage of boys and girls. About one in three of the drinkers drank one or more glasses of wine during an average week. Among the nondrinkers, boys and girls exhibited the same pattern of use they reported for beer.

Whisky and mixed drinks are the beverages least frequently drunk by the users. About one in four of the boy drinkers indicated that they drink one or more "shot" glasses (jiggers, probably about 1 oz.) of whisky or highballs during an average week. Only a slightly smaller number of the girls in this category drank this amount. As in the case of wine, the boys were more likely than the girls to consume larger amounts.

One in six of the boy drinkers had one or more mixed drinks in an average week while almost one in four of the girls in this category reported this amount.

No distinctive pattern of use appears in the reports of nondrinkers about their consumption of whisky and mixed drinks. Only a small number of these reported regular use of these beverages. It should be noted, however, that a larger percentage of girl nondrinkers (8%) reported using mixed drinks than any other alcoholic beverages. In brief, about one in two boy drinkers reported the consumption of beer one or more times a week and about one in four of these indicated that they use wine, whisky, mixed drinks or a combination of them one or more times in the average week. About one in four girl drinkers revealed a pattern of drinking one or more of these beverages on the average of at least once a week.

On the basis of interview data the differences in patterns of usage are at least partially explained by three considerations: (*1*) the students indicated an awareness that whisky is "more powerful" than beer or wine; (*2*) beer, and to some extent wine, is a common beverage in many homes, is on sale in most grocery stores and is, therefore, most accessible to them; (*3*) there is a slight but identifiable association on the part of the students between masculinity and the use of beer and whisky, and between femininity and the use of wine and mixed drinks.

Attention should be called to the large number of users who never, or rarely, drink beer during an average week, in spite of the fact that beer is the most commonly used beverage. This underscores the observation earlier that among teen-agers who drink, those who drink frequently and extensively are a small minority.

Occasions for Drinking

All the students, regardless of sex, use, or self-designation as drinker and nondrinker, essentially agreed that the most likely occasion for teen-age drinking is at a party, particularly a "wild," "beer" or "unsupervised" party (Table 2). This association between drinking and the "wild" party is especially pronounced among girls. Drinking among the teen-agers is not closely associated by these students with entertaining in the home, with school activities, or with occasions on which adults or relatives are drinking. Rather, the most likely drinking occasion is found at a party attended only by teen-agers.

The most commonly reported occasions on which students are most likely to drink are when with a group of age peers at a party where others are drinking, or in connection with special events or

TABLE 2.—*Responses to, "What Are the Three Most Likely Occasions for Drinking among Teen-Agers in High School?" By Use, Self-Designation and Sex, in Per Cent**

	Nonusers		*Users*			
			Nondrinkers		Drinkers	
Occasions	*Boys*	*Girls*	*Boys*	*Girls*	*Boys*	*Girls*
Party or dance	18	12	11	17	11	5
"Wild," "unsupervised," "beer," etc., party	45	59	45	45	38	60
Social visits among kinsmen or friends	14	10	3	8	6	5
Weddings, holidays	8	11	7	8	6	6
Other	15	8	34	22	39	24
Totals	*100*	*100*	*100*	*100*	*100*	*100*

* The total number of times a type of occasion was mentioned as one of the three responses is expressed as a percentage of the total of responses to the question.

TABLE 3.—*Responses of Users to, "Which of the Following Best Describe(s) the Situation in Which You Drink?" By Self-Designation and Sex, in Per Cent**

Situations	Nondrinkers *Boys*	Nondrinkers *Girls*	Drinkers *Boys*	Drinkers *Girls*
With a gang of friends	22	10	23	21
At parties where others drink	24	32	23	17
With parents or relatives	16	20	18	33
Special events or holidays	25	33	21	20
Fishing or hunting trips	10	2	8	2
Weekend recreation	0	3	7	6
Anywhere, anytime	3	0	†	1
Totals	*100*	*100*	*100*	*100*

* Multiple responses are included in these distributions. The total number of times a type of situation was mentioned is expressed as a percentage of the total number of responses to the question.

† Less than 1%.

holidays (Table 3). While drinking with age peers is prominently reported, specific or implicit inclusion of parents or other adult figures in situations in which the teen-ager drinks should be noted. Girls, moreover, were more likely than boys to describe the presence of parents or relatives who were drinking as occasions for their own drinking. Boys, on the other hand, were more likely than girls to report fishing or hunting trips as occasions. These reflect aspects of distinctly different patterns of drinking reported by boy and girl teen-agers.

Among nonusers, both boys (56%) and girls (67%) were more likely to have "tasted" alcohol on occasions when adults or relatives were drinking than at any other time (Table 4). The next most frequent response by boys in this category was "with a group of

TABLE 4.—*Responses to, "If You Do Not Drink But Have Tasted Alcohol, Which of the Following Best Describe(s) the Situation in Which You Have Tasted Alcohol?" By Sex, in Per Cent**

Situations	*Boys*	*Girls*
With a group of friends	18	7
At parties where others drink	6	4
With parents or relatives	56	67
Special events or holidays	12	20
Hunting or fishing trip	8	2
Totals	*100*	*100*

* Multiple responses are included in these distributions. The total number of times a type of situation was mentioned is expressed as a percentage of the total number of responses to the question.

friends" (18%), and by girls, at "special events" (20%). As on the reported occasions for drinking by boy and girl users, girl nonusers were more likely than boys to report the drinking of parents and relatives and less likely to indicate peer group situations as occasions for their "tasting."

These teen-age users, therefore, were more likely than nonusers to indicate peer group situations as occasions for their drinking. Conversely, they were less likely to indicate situations in which parents or relatives are present as occasions for their own drinking, although adults were reportedly present in a number of instances. In each of these categories, distinct male and female patterns of drinking are identifiable. In each case the girls were more likely to report situations in which parents or adult relatives are present as the most likely drinking or "tasting" occasion for themselves. Boys were more likely to report peer group situations.

Places for Teen-age Drinking

There was essential agreement among both users and nonusers that teen-agers are most likely to drink at places removed from adult supervision and control (Table 5). The "unsupervised party," "in secret where others will not know," "in automobiles" and "on back roads" illustrate the most frequently indicated places. Although students in the interviews also consistently mentioned having their first drinking or "tasting" experiences in the home and in the presence of parents, they emphasized that the most likely places

TABLE 5.—*Responses to, "What Are the Three Places Teen-Agers in High School Are Most Likely to Drink?" By Use, Self-Designation and Sex, in Per Cent**

	Nonusers		*Users*			
			Nondrinkers		Drinkers	
Drinking Places	*Boys*	*Girls*	*Boys*	*Girls*	*Boys*	*Girls*
In homes	12	17	13	10	12	10
Bars, taverns, clubs	1	1	1	3	2	1
Where dances or parties are held	10	6	9	10	6	10
In secret, out-of-the-way places	52	66	45	51	54	57
All other	25	10	32	26	26	22
Totals	*100*	*100*	*100*	*100*	*100*	*100*

* Multiple responses are included in these distributions. The total number of times a type of place was mentioned is expressed as a percentage of the total number of responses to the question.

for teen-age drinking are those where adults are absent. The inconsistency is only apparent. Materials from the interviews suggest that it may be resolved, at least in part, by recognizing that (*1*) drinking—or as students typically said, "tasting"—alcohol at home with parents does not necessarily authorize drinking in peer group situations or indicate approval of teen-age drinking on the part of parents; (*2*) parents, if they allow their children to drink in their presence, typically allow children to use alcohol only as "tasters"; (*3*) the purchase of alcoholic beverages is illegal for persons under 21 years of age in the state of Michigan; and (*4*) unsupervised drinking is socially defined by parents as inappropriate behavior for adolescents. Thus, teen-agers were not in doubt about general parental disapproval of unsupervised teen-age drinking. Therefore, if the teen-ager drinks with peers, he typically must do so in situations not controlled by adults. He may, however, "taste" alcohol in the presence of adults.

Summary.—Most teen-agers in this study did not use beverage alcohol and when they did, they did not do so frequently or in quantity. Almost all of them, however, had at one time or another had some limited experience with alcohol. About one out of four reported that they were not abstainers, though only about one in ten of all students and only two out of five of the users, designated themselves as drinkers. Beer was the beverage most frequently reported; yet among users this typically involved only one bottle of beer during the average week.

Slight but consistent sex differences were noted in the reports of alcoholic beverages used. Boys were more likely than girls to use beer and whisky; girls were likely to use wine and mixed drinks.

For users the most likely occasion for drinking was at a party attended by their peers and not supervised by adults. For nonusers generally, and for all girls to a greater extent than for boys, drinking occasions were most likely to be special events celebrated in the context of the home or with adults present. The presence of an adult on those occasions when teen-age drinking is permitted did not appear to indicate to the teen-agers that adults approve of their drinking without reservation; they did not interpret adult attitudes in this way at all. This is best indicated by the agreement of all the teen-agers in the study that teen-age drinking is ordinarily secretive. It is important to recognize that the purchase of alcoholic beverages on the part of these adolescents is illegal and this colors their thinking about alcohol use. Moreover, neither parents nor the formal institutions of social control in the adult society at large usually permit the teen-ager to assume adult status or play adult roles where drinking or abstinence are matters of personal discretion. These teen-agers gave no indication of assuming that adult attitudes favor unsupervised or unrestricted drinking. The students were aware of adult disapproval of their drinking, in contrast to "tasting." The consequent pressure to hide their drinking behavior suggests that peer groups are important to the adolescent (*1*) in freeing him somewhat from the adult-imposed notions of proper timing of alcohol use and (*2*) in providing support for experimentation with playing adult roles which from the standpoint of adults seem premature.

Community Social Structure, Drinking and Abstinence

Social interaction among individuals is not ordinarily a matter of chance. Individuals usually participate in and are members of social groups whose standardized symbols of communication allow them to place themselves in relation to others and to anticipate what is likely to happen in any given social situation. Group life is structured and organized to facilitate the accomplishment of those tasks and the achievement of those goals or values which are considered important by members of a group. The shared rules of behavior (social norms) which come to order the common ways of interaction within groups provide a basis for shared expectations about appropriate behavior.

Individuals may be placed or place themselves (*1*) formally in a group (e.g., doctor, father), (*2*) in terms of an informally defined interpersonal relationship (e.g., friend, one of the gang), (*3*) in terms of some particular value or disvalue (e.g., patriot, drinker), or in a combination of categories. Some of the factors involved in this positioning are ascribed at birth (e.g., race and sex) or are closely related to the biological development of the individual (e.g., age), while others are primarily achieved (e.g., occupation, education). The joining of a position with a definition of appropriate and expected behavior in given social situations is conveniently designated by the concepts *status* and *role*.

How one comes to recognize and identify oneself and others with various roles is fundamentally a matter of learning. One learns the traditional expectations about behavior characteristic of the groups which are relevant for him as these expectations are interpreted by both the statements and the behavior of others. One learns, for example, that all individuals do not play identical roles, and that the playing of some roles by certain individuals is sometimes required or encouraged, and at other times, discouraged or prohibited. But even persons who are presumably playing the same roles do not necessarily interpret the expectations identically; they also may sometimes presume to play certain roles in spite of discouragement or prohibition from other members of the group. The teen-age adolescent, for example, typically is not permitted to play some roles reserved for adults but may only "play at" them. This obviously does not mean, however, that no teen-agers prematurely claim the right to play or actually play some adult roles. Some teen-agers do. Drinking is a case in point.

The drinking behavior or abstinence of the adolescent cannot be understood without recognition of the position which he occupies in relevant social groups and how he conceives the roles associated with that position. The discussion which follows in the remainder of this chapter will consider specifically how three important aspects related to the positioning of an individual—sex, age, and socioeconomic status—are related to patterns of teen-age drinking and abstinence.

The starting point for age–sex differentiations and the practical justifications for them lie in the differing social potentialities of men and women at every age level. Social definitions of what it means to be male or female are involved in addition to biological differences. Some sex and age categories are recognized in all societies; for example, infant boy or girl, adult man or woman, old man or woman. Moreover, definitions of appropriate behavior of the young man and woman characteristically anticipate cultural definitions of appropriate adult behavior of men and women which adults share.

In addition to prescribing certain occupational and behavioral expectations, assignment to and membership in a particular age–sex group provide an individual with patterns for the proper behavior in his relationships with members of other age–sex groups (51). Consequently, the following paragraphs depict successively those aspects of sex and age in American social structure which have relevance for understanding the patterns of teen-age drinking and abstinence. The relationship between the patterns of drinking or abstinence and the socioeconomic status in the community, both the status of the teen-ager's family and his own status aspirations and expectations, will also be considered.

Sex Identification and Alcohol

The importance of sex differences in the pattern of response to alcohol use among teen-agers is illustrated by the relationships between sex and both the use of alcohol and choice of self-designations. Boys, for example, were much more likely to designate themselves as drinkers and to be users than were girls (Table 6). Among users, the percentage of boys is greater among drinkers than among nondrinkers. This same point may be made in another way. Forty-six per cent of the students in this study are boys, 54% girls. If the estimated sex distribution of nonusers presented in Table 6 is used, it is found that 67% of the boys are nonusers, 33% users. Among the users, 19% designated themselves as nondrinkers and 14% as drinkers. Correspondingly, 85% of the girls are nonusers, 15% users. Among the users, 10% designated themselves as nondrinkers and 5% as drinkers.

The sex differences in the pattern of teen-age drinking apparently reflect a basic distinction, of which drinking is only one aspect, between male and female roles which adults in our society also make. Surveys of adult drinking behavior in the United States consistently report that more women than men are abstainers and that women drinkers report drinking less.[4] Not only is drinking

TABLE 6.—*Designation of Self as "Drinker" or "Nondrinker," By Sex and Reported Use, in Per Cent*

	Nonusers	*Users*	
Sex		Nondrinkers	Drinkers
Male	39	62	73
Female	61	38	27
Totals	*100*	*100*	*100*
N	265	279	177

[4] Riley and Marden (71), using data based on a representative sample of the adult population in the United States, developed by the National Opinion Research Center, found that one in two women in contrast to one in four men were abstainers. These data have been corroborated by studies in single states (58, 64). Straus and Bacon (82) found twice as many women as men abstainers in a comprehensive study of drinking behavior in American colleges.

behavior of men and women in the United States different, it is also expected to be different. With drinking, as in other kinds of behavior, the American woman is subjected to a double standard.[5] The different cultural definitions of appropriate male and female behavior with regard to the use of alcohol observed in the larger society are reflected in what the teen-agers themselves say.

Although some teen-agers specifically rejected the "rightness" of a double standard for the drinking behavior of men and women, all of them recognized it as operative among both teen-agers and adults. One adolescent drinker said, for example:

"I think I would be embarrassed if my girl drank even if I were drinking. And the same way when they [girls] smoke. I don't think it looks right. But I think some girls expect their boy friends to smoke. I don't know why but I think that's right because boys—they expect it—oh, I don't know whether you would say rugged, go out and do things just for fun where girls—well, it just doesn't look right for her to do it."

In spite of the difficulty in articulating his feelings, this student was able to put across his point: Some behavior just "doesn't look right" for the girl and drinking is such behavior. Even a girl drinker with an equalitarian orientation who thought, "if [drinking] is good enough for a boy it is good enough for a girl," nevertheless observed, "I think a lot of people, even the police, don't think it's as bad for a boy as a girl to drink, but I don't know why that is. Maybe they feel that a girl can get carried away too far. . . ."

The two points illustrated in these excerpts from interviews were frequently echoed in the comments of other students. How basic this view is is reflected in the fact that recognition of felt differences in expectations for boys and girls were often accompanied by "I don't know why."

The students tended to circumscribe rather narrowly the situations in which drinking by girls is appropriate, if at all. As noted in the previous discussion of the places where teen-agers drink, the girl is more likely than the boy to associate drinking by girls with

[5] The notion of a "double standard," especially when applied in discussions of morality, frequently implies an unequal treatment of presumed equals. The presumption that men and women are equal is consistent with a strong equalitarian bias often encountered in the writing of Americans. It is not the point here to argue whether or not men and women are actually equal in some absolute sense. The important point is that the cultural definitions of appropriate male and female roles in our society are defined as different. From this point of view a "double standard" is adequately described as a different cultural definition of male and female roles. See, for example, Parsons (67) and Mead (59, *pp. 184-285*).

the home or with situations in which parents or relatives are present. Although the boy was likely to say that drinking by girls "just doesn't look right," no comparable statement was applied by girls to males in general. One explanation of the different assessments by students of the appropriateness of male and female drinking behavior is found in the association between the willingness of the girl to drink outside the home and moral laxity. "It's okay," said one boy, "if you are going to pick up girls someplace if they drink; but for the one that you really decide to marry—well, they wouldn't go." A girl nondrinker also observed, "Parents are more concerned about girls than boys because they know they expect a certain amount of devil from boys but not from girls. . . . Parents don't even like to see their girls smoke."

Definitions of appropriate male and appropriate female behavior with regard to the use of beverage alcohol are widely shared within the social groups in which these high-school students participate. The difference in expectations is reflected both in what the students do with alcohol and in what they say about the appropriateness of that behavior. The students' definitions as well as their behavior appear to be similar to and to reflect adult role definitions and role behavior involving the use of alcohol.

Age Grading, Drinking and Abstinence

Age as well as sex is associated with differences in expectations about alcohol use, in reported use, and in preferences for identification as a drinker or nondrinker. S. N. Eisenstadt (18, 20) in an analysis of certain African societies characterized by social groups based on age, has discussed the importance of age grading for understanding behavior. He concludes that distinct age grades arise and have particular significance in situations where rules of social interaction are not overwhelmingly determined by membership in kinship groups. In such situations important interpretations of appropriate behavior are made by groups composed of adolescent peers as well as by family members. These interpretations by groups of the adolescent's peers provide for continuity and stability in the socialization process when stringent kinship controls are absent. In such situations groups of adolescents may provide an important bridge between family groups and the larger society.[6]

[6] The functions of age peer groups in facilitating the acculturation of the children of foreign-born parents in the United States has often been noted. This situation

In our own society groups are not usually based on formal age categorization except in the educational system. Nevertheless, groups based on age are an integral part of our social structure and constitute an important point of reference for understanding kinship structure, organization of formal education, occupational preparation, and community participation. Although in most cases the lines separating age grades are not rigidly specified, this does not lessen the importance of these distinctions (67). In fact, it is this combination of the importance attached to age differences and the lack of specificity in delimiting the various age grades that is of special interest in American society. Many societies provide rites of passage which clearly demarcate the transition from one age grade to another, particularly the transition from childhood to adulthood. In our society, however, there are only a few rudimentary equivalents of rites of passage marking the achievement of adult status. Such rites of passage as these are seen in the coming out party of the upper-class girl and in such varied events as high-school graduation, being inducted into the Armed Forces, the legal age for voting, or taking a full-time job and marriage (94, *pp. 71*).

Although specific criteria for delimiting age grades are few, our public school system illustrates an age graded social organization. Robert J. Havighurst (33), for example, has divided the process of growing up in American society into four stages, each lasting about six years and focused around movement through the educational system. The first period, ages 1 to 6, is pre-school; the second, ages 6 to 12, is the first 6 grades in our school system; the third, ages 12 to 18, is normally junior or senior high school and roughly corresponds with adolescence; the fourth, ages 18 through 21—the period after graduation from high school—is identified with young adulthood.

Each of these periods has associated with it certain culturally defined tasks or goals. For our present purpose it is sufficient to concentrate on the tasks of adolescence, the age period which includes the high-school students used in our study of teen-age drink-

illustrates in extreme form the importance of peer groups in bridging the gap between family training and acquiring the social skills required for adequate participation in the host society. In courtship and marriage, social and political beliefs and behavior, and in occupational selection, the peer group has frequently had a marked influence on the behavior of its members. See, for example, Sneidler and Ravitz (78).

ing behavior. These tasks, according to Havighurst, are (*1*) accepting one's physique and the appropriate masculine or feminine role; (*2*) achieving new relations with age-mates of both sexes; (*3*) achieving emotional independence of parents and other adults; (*4*) achieving assurance of economic independence; (*5*) selecting and preparing for an occupation; (*6*) developing intellectual skills and concepts necessary for civic competence; (*7*) desiring and achieving socially responsible behavior; (*8*) preparing for marriage and family life; and (*9*) building conscious values (esthetic, religious, ethical) in harmony with an adequate scientific world-picture. In brief, the peculiar problems of adolescence are the achievement of ego identity and the development of the attitudes, knowledge and skills necessary to sustain this sense of identity (22, 24).

The coincidence of the importance attached to age grades and of the vagueness in delimiting them has provoked a great deal of discussion about the ambiguous situation thus created for young people. An example is Talcott Parsons' contention that, out of this ambiguity a "youth culture" emerges (67, 69). This subculture which develops among the young is characterized by social expectations and patterns of behavior which involve highly complex combinations of age grading and sex role elements. Parsons' point of view is shared by a large number of observers who characteristically view the adolescent period of development as stormy and stressful as well as a period dominated by a distinctive peer group culture.[7] Three major assumptions appear to be implicit in this characterization of adolescence: (*1*) Adolescence is assumed to be a unique period in which "storm and stress" inevitably result from the adolescent's peculiar position in an age graded social structure. The discontinuities in expectations about appropriate behavior, the conflict between the perspectives of different generations in a changing society, and the problems associated with occupational and marital choice are all said to contribute to the tensions of the adolescent. (*2*) A second assumption is that a youth culture not only exists but also is a widespread and dominant pattern among adolescents in American life, particularly in urban areas. Those who participate in this culture are said to experience its demands, to accept its dominant elements and to judge their

[7] For a summary of this characterization and a critique of it, see Elkin and Westley (21).

behavior by peer-group standards rather than by adult standards. (3) Finally, it is assumed that the youth culture of the adolescent occasions and encourages the "storm and stress" experienced by young people. An adolescent, in becoming emancipated from his family, participates in a peer group which makes demands to which he tends to conform; and in so doing he meets in part his needs for both independence and security.

The extent to which adolescents in general participate in and are influenced by such a youth culture as characterized above is problematic. So is the relevance of such a subculture for understanding and explaining teen-age drinking behavior. The research reported provides a basis for inquiring about the relationship between age and patterns of response to alcohol use among the teen-agers of a particular community. The thesis to be developed here is that teen-agers perceive some drinking to be characteristic of adult behavior; the more closely the teen-ager is identified with adult status by age, by the experience of personal autonomy and responsibility in decision making, and by the opportunity to play adult roles, the more likely he is to identify himself as a drinker and to use beverage alcohol. Thus the influence of age peers, while perhaps important in determining the specific timing and occasions for some drinking among teen-agers, is less important than the teen-agers' perception of alcohol use as an integral part of adult behavior.

Age Grades and Perceptions of Drinking Behavior

These adolescents perceived drinking to be common behavior among adults but not among their age peers. Regardless of the self-designation of the student as a drinker or nondrinker, two-thirds or more of them estimated that at least half of the adult population drink "sometimes" (Table 7). When estimates are considered separately by self-designation and by sex, the proportion of students in each category making this estimate ranged from a low of 67% of the nonusers to a high of 74% of the girl nondrinkers among the users.

About half of the students also estimated that at least half the adult population drink "regularly" (Table 7). The proportion of students in each category making this estimate ranged from a low of 49% of the nonusers to a high of 61% of the boy drinkers. A slight but consistent tendency for users, in contrast to nonusers,

TABLE 7.—*Estimates By Teen-Agers of the Proportion of Adults Who Drink "Sometimes" and "Regularly," By Use, Self-Designation and Sex, in Per Cent*

	Nonusers		*Users*			
			Nondrinkers		Drinkers	
Sometimes	*Boys*	*Girls*	*Boys*	*Girls*	*Boys*	*Girls*
Less than half	27	29	23	22	27	29
Half or more	67	67	73	74	71	69
Do not know	6	4	4	4	2	2
Totals	*100*	*100*	*100*	*100*	*100*	*100*
Regularly						
Less than half	45	47	41	39	37	48
Half or more	49	49	54	58	61	50
Do not know	6	4	5	2	2	2
Totals	*100*	*100*	*100*	*100*	*100*	*100*
N	104	161	172	107	129	48

to make higher estimates of the proportion of adults who drink is apparent.

While the students in the study tended to perceive the adult as a person who drinks at least sometimes, their perceptions of adolescent behavior were less in agreement. A majority of nonusers (65%) estimated that less than half of their age peers drink even sometimes. Among the users, only the boy nondrinkers agreed (Table 8). All the students agreed, however, that a majority of high-school students do not drink "regularly" (Table 8). In Table 8 a pronounced tendency for users, in contrast to nonusers, to make higher estimates of the number of their peers who drink is evident. Among

TABLE 8.—*Estimates of the Proportion of High-School Students Who Drink "Sometimes" and "Regularly," By Use, Self-Designation and Sex, in Per Cent*

	Nonusers		*Users*			
			Nondrinkers		Drinkers	
Sometimes	*Boys*	*Girls*	*Boys*	*Girls*	*Boys*	*Girls*
Less than half	66	65	56	2	43	44
Half or more	29	30	40	93	55	54
Do not know	5	5	4	5	2	2
Totals	*100*	*100*	*100*	*100*	*100*	*100*
Regularly						
Less than half	80	75	79	67	63	56
Half or more	12	22	14	32	35	42
Do not know	8	3	7	1	2	2
Totals	*100*	*100*	*100*	*100*	*100*	*100*
N	104	161	172	107	129	48

users, the drinkers consistently made higher estimates than the nondrinkers. Thus in the various estimates of the proportion of adults and high-school students who drink, the students tend to maximize the number of persons whose behavior is presumably most like their own. Perceptions of the occasions and places for adult drinking were quite similar among the various students. Composite responses to the question, "What are the three occasions on which adults are most likely to drink?" indicate that social situations are consistently ranked high (Table 9). All students, regardless of use, self-designation or sex, perceived convivial social activity such as a party or dance as an occasion for drinking by adults. They also agreed that this drinking is most likely to occur on special occasions such as New Year's, Christmas and other holidays, and when adults are entertaining friends or kinsmen at home. Two-thirds or more of the responses of each category of students is accounted for by such occasions. Thus the teen-agers perceived adult drinking to be in the context of normal social acti-

TABLE 9.—*Responses to, "What Are the Three Occasions When, and the Three Places Where, Adults Are Most Likely to Drink?" By Use, Self-Designation and Sex, in Per Cent**

	Nonusers		*Users*			
			Nondrinkers		Drinkers	
Drinking Occasions	*Boys*	*Girls*	*Boys*	*Girls*	*Boys*	*Girls*
Party or dance	26	22	24	23	29	26
"Wild," "unsupervised," "beer," etc., party	2	1	2	2	2	1
Social visits among kinsmen or friends	25	17	17	18	15	20
Weddings, holidays	27	29	21	26	23	26
Other	20	31	36	31	31	27
Totals	*100*	*100*	*100*	*100*	*100*	*100*
Drinking Places						
In homes	42	47	41	45	39	44
Bars, taverns, clubs	26	33	26	22	23	22
Where dances or parties are held	9	15	8	12	12	12
In secret out-of-the-way places	†	0	2	1	2	3
Other	23	5	23	20	24	19
Totals	*100**	*100*	*100*	*100*	*100*	*100*

* Multiple responses are included in these distributions. The total number of times a type of place was mentioned is expressed as a percentage of the total number of responses to the question.
† Less than 1%.

vities, in sharp contrast to the occasions for drinking they perceive to be characteristic of teen-agers.

When the occasions for adult drinking are compared with those occasions most likely to elicit student drinking (see Table 2), it is noted that "party" is most frequently mentioned in each instance. However, there is a difference. In the case of the teen-ager, a prefix such as "wild," "unsupervised," or "beer" is added.

Students in all categories also agree that adult drinking is most likely to occur in such public places as bars, clubs or taverns and in social activities centering in the home (Table 9). Nonpublic places which imply secretive behavior are not associated with adult drinking. This is in contrast to the teen-ager's designation of secret or unsupervised places as the most likely for drinking by students (see Table 5), such as "at unsupervised parties," "in automobiles," or "on back roads."

Age Grading and Reference Groups

Because of these different perceptions of adolescent and adult drinking behavior, a teen-ager's identification with either adolescents or adults is related both to his reaction to the use of alcohol and to his own self-conception as a drinker or a nondrinker. The propositions developed here are that (*1*) the older the student the more likely he is to be a user and, if a user, to identify himself as a drinker; and (*2*) the greater the identification and experience with adult roles and the greater the expectation of achieving adult status immediately after graduation from high school, the more likelihood that a student will be a user and, if a user, will identify himself as a drinker.

Users were found to be older than nonusers, and self-designated drinkers older than nondrinkers (Table 10). Thus older teen-agers,

TABLE 10.—*Age of Users and Nonusers, in Per Cent*

	Nonusers		*Users*			
			Nondrinkers		Drinkers	
Age in Years	*Boys*	*Girls*	*Boys*	*Girls*	*Boys*	*Girls*
16 or younger	31	51	32	40	1	6
17	42	39	43	39	23	38
18 or older	25	8	23	20	71	54
No answer	2	2	2	1	5	2
Totals	*100*	*100*	*100*	*100*	*100*	*100*
N	104	161	172	107	129	48

those who were approaching an age when claims to adult status are increasingly feasible, were more likely than younger ones to indicate an acceptance of alcohol use. The association between increasing age and the probability that a student would be a user can be illustrated in another way. If an estimate of the age distribution of the boy nonusers is made, it is found that the percentage of nonusers among boys 16 years old or younger is 74%; among the 17-year-olds it is 71%; but among those 18 years old and over, the percentage of nonusers decreases to 53%. Similarly, among girls, the percentage of nonusers decreases from 91% of those 16 years old or younger, to 86% of the 17-year-olds, to 61% of those 18 and older.

Since the achievement of personal identity and the interpersonal competence necessary to maintain that identity is one of the basic tasks of the adolescent approaching young adulthood, the teen years are a time of increasing independence from adult supervision and of increasingly frequent assertions of personal autonomy. It should follow then, that teen-agers who are most advanced in the achievement of personal autonomy would not only be older but also be most likely to use adult roles as points of reference. And, insofar as the adult is perceived as likely to be a drinker, these students should also be more likely than others to be users and to identify themselves as drinkers. The data tend to support this interpretation.

Most students reported that they live with both their parents. In such situations they are likely to be defined as children, not the young adult peers of their parents. On the other hand, one might expect that, in the absence of a parent of the same sex, a child would have the occasion if not the necessity to play adult roles sooner than he might ordinarily. Among boys living in family units in which the father was present 68% were nonusers, as compared with 53% living in units in which the father was absent. Correspondingly, 87% of the girls living with their mothers were nonusers, compared with 77% of those whose mothers were absent. Whether this relationship is to be explained in terms of accelerated achievement of emotional and economic independence, of pressure to assume adult responsibility for self or others, of differences in parental control, or of a combination of these cannot be answered from these data.

Money is purchasing power and purchasing power is, to some extent, discretionary power. One facet of the individual's achievement of increasing autonomy, therefore, lies in having access to money not directly subject to parental control. One source of such money for a teen-ager is provided by earnings from work away from home. If users, as we have argued, are more likely than others to identify themselves with adult roles, then one would expect them to have greater access to financial resources which permit the autonomy in decision making associated with adulthood. This is found to be the case (Table 11), although the difference between users and nonusers in this instance is minimal. For both boys and girls users are more likely than nonusers to have access to money not directly subject to parental control. Since the right to make one's own decisions and the availability of the economic resources to implement these decisions is associated with adulthood, the achievement of some measure of financial independence does make independent decisions, including decisions about drinking, increasingly a live option for the working teen-ager. It is important to note also that working outside the home, in addition to providing an independent source of income, provides the teen-ager with the opportunity to observe at close range other adults playing and interpreting adult roles.

Users and drinkers are not only more likely than others to have experience in jobs outside the home; they also are more likely to have plans for the assumption of adult-role responsibilities immediately after high school (Table 12). Nonusers tend to be oriented toward college, users toward the full-time job or enlistment in the armed services, both of which are associated with adult role playing: an estimated 77% of the boys and 92% of the girls planning to attend college are nonusers, compared with 58% of the

TABLE 11.—*Experience in Earning Money By Working at Home and Away From Home, in Per Cent*

	Nonusers		*Users*			
			Nondrinkers		Drinkers	
Experience in Earning	*Boys*	*Girls*	*Boys*	*Girls*	*Boys*	*Girls*
Never or hardly ever	9	19	8	19	5	8
Yes, work at home	13	18	15	17	8	13
Yes, work away from home	78	61	76	64	86	77
No answer	0	1	1	0	1	2
Totals	*100*	*100*	*100*	*100*	*100*	*100*
N	104	161	172	107	129	48

TABLE 12.—*Plans Following High School, By Use, Self-Designation and Sex, in Per Cent*

	Nonusers		*Users*			
			Nondrinkers		Drinkers	
Plans	*Boys*	*Girls*	*Boys*	*Girls*	*Boys*	*Girls*
College	47	36	26	16	32	19
Vocational school	2	12	10	14	5	12
Full-time job	15	39	20	50	19	53
Armed service	23	7	35	9	35	8
Uncertain	13	6	9	11	9	8
Totals	*100*	*100*	*100*	*100*	*100*	*100*
N	104	161	172	107	129	48

boys and 82% of the girls planning to enter the work force or armed forces.

Differences in the importance which users and nonusers attach to adolescent peer groups would also be expected if the proposition being developed here is correct. Users are, in fact, found to be less oriented than others to organized activities involving teen-age peers (Table 13). This difference is reflected both in the higher proportion of users who participate in no high-school organization and in the smaller number of organizations to which those who do participate belong.

When organized nonschool activities are considered, nonusers are again less likely than users to report no participation (Table 14). Among boy participants, users are generally less active than nonusers in all types of activities except group sports. Among girls, users are less likely than nonusers to participate in all types of organized nonschool activities. Moreover, the users, in spite of being less active than others, were no more inclined than the nonusers, in fact were slightly less inclined, to increase their participation (Table 15).

TABLE 13.—*Participation in High-School Organizations By Use, Self-Designation and Sex*

	Nonusers		*Users*			
			Nondrinkers		Drinkers	
	Boys	*Girls*	*Boys*	*Girls*	*Boys*	*Girls*
Participate in no organization	30%	16%	51%	22%	44%	21%
Median number of organizations	1.7	2.0	1.0	1.3	1.3	1.1

TABLE 14.—*Student Participation in Nonschool Activities, By Use, Self-Designation and Sex, in Per Cent*[*]

	Nonusers		*Users*			
			Nondrinkers		Drinkers	
Activity	*Boys*	*Girls*	*Boys*	*Girls*	*Boys*	*Girls*
Group sports	24	18	32	16	24	13
Young peoples' religious group	23	29	11	20	10	21
Musical or artistic group	9	12	5	8	3	13
Community activities	7	11	7	9	9	10
Boy or girl scouts	4	3	6	2	7	3
None	33	27	40	45	47	40
Totals	*100*	*100*	*100*	*100*	*100*	*100*

[*] Multiple responses are included in all totals. The number of times a type of response was given is expressed as a percentage of the total number of responses.

These data suggest the need to make a basic distinction among various teen-age groups with regard to drinking. Since users, and even more so the self-designated drinkers, constitute a minority of students in the study and report participating least in organized group activity both inside and outside the school, it would not be warranted to maintain that adolescent groups in general are a source of support for drinking. On the contrary, most students perceived adolescents as abstinent, suggesting just the opposite. In a minority of cases, peer group participation may be important in the development and support of the self- and social conception of drinker. But more important, it appears that those groups in which the user participates are composed of those teen-agers who are older, have achieved some financial independence, have more immediate plans for establishing themselves occupationally, prefer adult models of behavior and are least involved in the organized teen-age activities either inside or outside the school.

In sum, the user, and particularly the self-designated drinker,

TABLE 15.—*Total Number of Team Memberships, Organizations and Activities Desired By Students, By Use, Self-Designation and Sex*

	Nonusers		*Users*			
			Nondrinkers		Drinkers	
	Boys	*Girls*	*Boys*	*Girls*	*Boys*	*Girls*
Percentage desiring no participation	51%	63%	51%	61%	62%	67%
Median number of memberships desired, if any	0.90	0.79	0.98	0.82	0.81	0.75
N	104	161	172	107	129	48

appears most likely to be the teen-ager who is playing essentially adult roles and whose preferred groups are composed either of adults or of other teen-agers whose behavior identifies them with adult status. There was no indication from the responses of these students that most teen-agers or teen-age peer groups in these high schools are basically antagonistic to perceived adult definitions of the inappropriateness of drinking by adolescents. Nor was there any indication in the interviews that "storm and stress" surrounded the issue of drinking for these older adolescents. Rather, it was those students apparently most advanced in the assumption of adult roles who were most likely to drink and to designate themselves as drinkers.

Relevance of Social Stratification for Drinking Behavior[8]

Socioeconomic stratification may be observed as a part of the organized social life in any American community. Although the details vary from one society to another, power, prestige, and life chances are never equally distributed among individuals. These differences may be reflected in the distribution of such social rewards as income, occupational prestige, social honor, educational opportunity, or some other combination of factors which reflect group values. Differences in socioeconomic position are also reflected in the preferences which people have for associating with others who have the same or a similar status position in a community.

When groups of people have, or are thought to have, the same or similar socioeconomic positions within a community, these groups are referred to as classes and commonly designated as "upper," "middle" or "lower." Although these designations oversimplify a very complex social process,[9] for our purposes here they will serve adequately.

The information used in determining the socioeconomic placement of students was of four types. First, the father's occupation was used. This is one of the better simple indicators of a family's socioeconomic position; a child's status in a community, for example, largely reflects the status of the father.[10] The technique

[8] The discussion of social stratification in the following paragraphs draws especially on the work of Weber (92) and Warner, Meeker and Eells (89). See also the critical discussion of issues and bibliography in this field in Pfautz (70).

[9] For example, see Pfautz (70) and Stone and Form (80).

[10] See, for example, Kahl and Davis (42) and Parsons (66).

used to rank occupations was the United States Census classification of occupations. Second, a Warner Index of Status Characteristics was used to provide a gross estimate of social class position (89). The process by which this summary index of status is determined involves the conversion of weighted scales of occupation, source of income and education into a single index. This summary index permits the tentative placement of individuals within a framework of social classes. Third, the socioeconomic aspirations and expectations of the students were compared in terms of techniques discussed in the two previous points. Fourth, the interviews provided insight into the perceptions which students themselves have of social class in the community in which they live and the way in which the style of life in the various classes is related to drinking behavior. What the students had to say about social class and alcohol use provides a convenient place to begin.

Student Images of Social Class

When teen-agers themselves talked informally of socioeconomic distinctions in the interviews, they often referred to "upper class," "middle class," "lower class" or some variant of these. Class position was most frequently described by them in terms of differences in money, prestige, power and opportunity, as illustrated by the student who said:

"Class means whether you're the person who has the most money and has more opportunity—usually opportunity goes with money. Or, if you're the lower class you don't have opportunity or money. The middle class may have to pinch pennies but still they get along."

How is class position related to drinking behavior? The response of one teen-ager summarized with insight the less explicit comments made often by other students in the interviews:

"I think all groups drink, but the older group and the older society groups and the high-ups in society drink as much as the lower group but drink a better quality of stuff and know when to stop and can consume it better. The lower class group of people drink a lot and don't know when to stop and are boisterous about it. . . . In between I think they drink just mildly and they drink when they want to and where they want to and know how much to drink and when to stop and when not to and things like that. High society people, they feel, they—oh, I don't know, I'm not high society—but they are drinking and I think they can drink a lot. They're used to the different parties and can drink any place they want. I don't think they get out of hand because they are afraid they'll lose their society. . . . The people at the bottom, they don't care, because they don't have any place else to fall; they can just fall where they are. The middle class are in between. They know whether to drink and when to drink and how to drink."

The students frequently pointed out that drinking is likely to be part of a style of life, particularly among the "upper class." "Social drinking" was commonly used to describe the behavior of this category of persons. On the other hand, drinking by "lower class" persons was likely to be thought of as one mechanism for escape from personal problems or worry. Some students were also inclined to moralize that "if a fellow is in a lower class and is spending all his money for liquor, that's probably why he is in the lower class."[11] In brief, the students interviewed shared an identifiable image of the relationship between socioeconomic position in the community and drinking behavior. Analysis of what they reported on the questionnaires lends support to these impressions from the interviews.

Socioeconomic Status of the Family

Users were not equally distributed throughout the range of socioeconomic status as defined by the occupations of fathers. Rather, they are concentrated at the lower end of the status continuum. Teen-agers classified in the lower socioeconomic strata of a community might be expected to have neither the resources nor the status aspirations to make the postponement of a full-time job, marriage, or entrance into the armed services a feasible or desirable option.[12] The postponement of full adult status by continuing professional or technical preparation is more likely to appear both possible and desirable among teen-agers from families with higher status.

As expected, when census classifications of the father's occupations are used, the users were concentrated in the lower occupational classifications (Table 16). Among boys, 54% of the nonusers had fathers in white-collar occupations (professionals, managers,

[11] The notion that the "upper class" drink like "ladies and gentlemen" in contrast to the more rowdy and less glamorous drinking among the "lower class" is reported in Dollard (17); for a characterization of drinking by the "country club crowd" in contrast to those who drink in roadhouses and bars see Hollingshead (36, *pp. 321 ff.*).

[12] Havighurst (33) develops this point of view in detail; see also Hyman (39).

TABLE 16.—*Father's Occupation (Census Classification), By Use, Self-Designation and Sex, in Per Cent*

	Nonusers		*Users*			
			Nondrinkers		Drinkers	
	Boys	*Girls*	*Boys*	*Girls*	*Boys*	*Girls*
Professional–managerial	39	34	21	15	15	23
Clerical–sales	15	9	16	8	18	10
Craftsmen–operatives	34	50	28	35	25	25
Other	12	7	35	42	42	42
Totals	*100*	*100*	*100*	*100*	*100*	*100*
N	104	161	172	107	129	48

clerks or salesmen) in contrast to the users among whom 63% of the nondrinkers and 67% of the drinkers had fathers employed in blue-collar occupations (craftsmen, operatives, service workers). A similar distribution is noted among the various categories of girls. Forty-three per cent of the nonusers reported the father to have a white-collar occupation. Among the users, in contrast, 23% of the nondrinkers and 33% of the drinkers made this report. Since the distribution of occupations among the random sample of nonusers approximates the distribution among all the nonusers among the students in the study, the relationship between the status of an adolescent's family and alcohol use can be illustrated in another way. Among boys, 75% of those with a father in a white-collar occupation were nonusers; 65% of the remaining boys were. Similarly, among relatively upper-status girls, 90% were nonusers; while among others, 82% were.

The Warner Index of Status Characteristics, because it includes education and source of income in addition to an evaluation of occupational status, is a more refined indicator of class than is the census classification of occupations alone. When students are placed in terms of social class based on the Warner Index, a modified picture of the relationship between drinking and class emerges (Table 17). Users are less clearly located in the lower range of the status structure than was the case when occupational classification of the father alone was used. The user was more likely than others to be found at the upper and lower extremes of the class structure. The nonuser, on the other hand, was most likely to be found in the middle range of status. Seventy per cent of the middle-class boys were nonusers in contrast to 63% of those in the

TABLE 17.—*Father's Social Class (Warner Index of Status Characteristics), By Use, Self-Designation and Sex, in Per Cent*

	Nonusers		*Users*			
			Nondrinkers		Drinkers	
	Boys	*Girls*	*Boys*	*Girls*	*Boys*	*Girls*
Upper class	2	0	0	0	5	6
Middle class	50	52	46	34	38	28
Lower class	42	41	42	60	44	57
Unclassified	6	7	12	6	13	8
Totals	*100*	*100*	*100*	*100*	*100*	*100*
N	104	161	172	107	129	48

upper class, 66% of those in the lower class, and 49% of those whose class position could not be classified because one or another crucial piece of information was not reported. Correspondingly, 91% of the middle-class girls, 80% of the lower-class, and no upper-class ones were nonusers.

Status Aspirations and Expectations

While an adolescent receives his socioeconomic position in the community from the status of the father, a young person may also aspire to and identify himself with a socioeconomic position he prefers as well as the one he himself expects to achieve as an adult. For example, the son of a factory operative may aspire to a professional occupation or to be in a social class higher than the one his family currently occupies. He may have as the preferred model of his behavior in such a case not his father but the image of an adult or adults occupying the status positions to which he aspires. A similar observation might be made of the girl whose status aspirations, which are expected to be realized in a career or in marriage, do not coincide with her present social status. The following paragraphs will explore the relevance of status aspirations vis-à-vis status expectations for understanding the drinking behavior of high-school teen-agers.

When the father's occupation is projected as a possible occupation for self or for husband, users were more likely than nonusers to evaluate this possibility as "poor" or "very poor" (Table 18). This is consistent with the observation that users are more likely than others to come from families in which the occupational status of the father is predominantly low. Among boys, 46% of the non-

TABLE 18.—*Student Estimates of Acceptability of Father's Occupation for Self or Spouse, By Use, Self-Designation and Sex, in Per Cent*

	Nonusers		*Users*			
			Nondrinkers		Drinkers	
Estimates	*Boys*	*Girls*	*Boys*	*Girls*	*Boys*	*Girls*
Good–very good	46	58	43	49	36	35
Fair	27	22	27	25	27	29
Poor–very poor	23	18	22	22	34	30
No answer	4	2	8	4	3	6
Totals	*100*	*100*	*100*	*100*	*100*	*100*
N	104	161	172	107	129	48

users considered the father's occupation as "good" or "very good" as a possibility for themselves in contrast to 36% of the drinkers and 43% of the nondrinkers. More than half of the girl nonusers considered the father's occupation as "good" or "very good" for themselves or their spouses in contrast to one in three of the drinkers and slightly less than half of the nondrinkers.

Users and nonusers had different occupational expectations. For example, among boys, 40% of the nonusers in contrast to 30% of the nondrinkers and 33% of the drinkers expected professional–managerial occupations for themselves (Table 19). When this expectation is compared with the reported occupational status of the father (Table 16), the number of nonusers expecting this classification is about equal to those whose fathers actually have this classification. The number of users expecting these occupational classifications, however, reflects upward occupational aspirations for many. Among nondrinkers, the number of students who expect top

TABLE 19.—*Students' Occupational Expectations for Self or Spouse, By Use, Self-Designation and Sex, in Per Cent*

	Nonusers		*Users*			
			Nondrinkers		Drinkers	
Expectations	*Boys*	*Girls*	*Boys*	*Girls*	*Boys*	*Girls*
Professional–managerial	40	30	30	16	33	29
Clerical–sales	3	33	4	37	2	23
Craftsman–operative	17	4	35	4	22	6
Other	5	6	6	19	4	8
No answer	35	27	25	24	39	34
Totals	*100*	*100*	*100*	*100*	*100*	*100*
N	104	161	172	107	129	48

level occupations was greater (30%) than the number reporting such occupations for the father (21%). Among drinkers the discrepancy is even greater (33% compared to 15%).

The differences between the expected (for self or spouse) and the reported occupational classification of the father among the boys are also found among the girls. Thirty per cent of the nonusers expected a professional or managerial occupation for self or spouse, while 16% of the nondrinkers and 29% of the drinkers had this expectation. Again the expectation of upward mobility is more apparent among the users (compare Table 16). On the assumption that the father's occupation is a fair indicator of a son's probable occupation or the probable occupation of a daughter's spouse, these students seem realistic in stating their occupational expectations.

As might be expected in a society in which white-collar jobs are available to women in increasing numbers and in which there is the general expectation that a woman should marry up the status ladder, all the girls expected upward social mobility. Sixty-three per cent of the nonusers, 53% of the nondrinkers and 52% of the drinkers expected a white-collar occupation for self or spouse. Of the girl nonusers, 21% more expected a white-collar occupation for self or spouse than had fathers in such occupations. Similar discrepancies of 16% and 19% were found among nondrinkers and drinkers, respectively.

Evidence of the relationship between class and use or nonuse of alcohol among these teen-agers in high school may be summed up as follows. When the occupation of the father alone serves as an indicator of status, users are more likely than others to come from a family in which the father has a blue-collar occupation. However, when additional criteria are used to place students in a hierarchy of social classes, users are more likely to be found in upper and lower classes, the nonusers in the middle class. Among boys, use of alcohol appears to be related to the preference and expectation of upward social mobility. Among girls, the relationship between potential upward social mobility and use of alcohol is less clear. Girl nonusers, however, are more likely than others to expect such mobility.

Among users, the nondrinkers and drinkers were not sharply differentiated from each other in terms of the various indicators of status used. Characteristically, however, in any comparison of status characteristics between nonusers and users the greatest differences were found between nonusers and the self-designated drinkers.

Summary

This chapter has concentrated on the patterns of teen-age drinking and abstinence. The focus of attention has been on the two acts: (*1*) the use or avoidance of alcohol; and (*2*) the self-designation of the *user* as *drinker* or *nondrinker*. A second focus has been on the location of the teen-agers in the community in terms of sex, age and socioeconomic status.

Most teen-agers in the study were found not to use alcohol either frequently or in quantity. Drinking for them was not experimental or occasional, as appears to be the case for most drinking nondrinkers. For the self-designated *drinker* the use of alcohol appeared to be a normal part of his behavior. He was most likely to drink with his peers in situations in which adults were absent, particularly at a party. The surreptitious aspects of his drinking behavior are in large part explained by the recognized disapproval of adolescent drinking by adults and his assumption that such behavior is generally disapproved in the community.

The North American adolescent occupies a somewhat anomalous position in our society. He is no longer a child but not quite an adult. Appropriate behavior for men and women is defined differently. Both these facts have significance for understanding his use or avoidance of alcohol. Regardless of use or nonuse of alcohol and of his self-designation as a *drinker* or a *nondrinker,* the teen-agers studied perceived the adult as a person who drinks at least sometimes. But only the *users* who designated themselves as *drinkers* perceived most other adolescents as persons who drink sometimes. This means that the teen-ager's conception of himself primarily as an adolescent or an adult should be closely related to his use or nonuse of alcohol and his self-designation as a *drinker* or *nondrinker*. The data tend to support this conclusion.

Those teen-agers who are older; who, for whatever reason, are playing or expect soon to play adult roles; who prefer adult models of behavior; and who are least active in organized teen-age activities—these are the teen-agers who are most likely to be *users* and, if *users,* to designate themselves as *drinkers.* While some teen-age peer groups in some cases support the *drinker's* conception of himself, this is clearly not the case for most teen-age peer groups. A distinctive widely shared "youth culture" supporting drinking among these adolescents is not apparent.

The *drinker* seems best described as a person whose preferred groups are primarily adult oriented. But the groups within which he interacts most frequently are necessarily largely composed of adolescents. His claims to adult status, or at least to the adult's right to discretion about his drinking or abstinence, are acknowledged by neither adults nor most other adolescents.

From the little evidence which is available on the drinking mores of the different classes in American society, it appears that drinking is most common among the "upper class" and the "lower class." The results of this study give tentative support to this observation. In addition, use of alcohol and the designation of self as a drinker is related to expectations of social mobility among boys. Whether or not this relationship can be explained in terms of the presumed ability of drinking to facilitate this mobility requires further investigation.

57

Chapter 4

[D]RINKING AND SOCIAL NORMS

OUR CULTURAL HERITAGE incorporates at least two diverse traditions about drinking. On the one hand, as McCarthy and Douglass noted, "Social tradition, economic competition and governmental practice provided the social sanctions for the production and consumption of alcoholic beverages in early America. By the beginning of the nineteenth century the new nation had established a reputation as a hard-drinking people" (55, *p. 12*).[1] Research indicates that in the twentieth century drinking is still widespread.[2]

On the other hand, the temperance movement in the United States has a history almost as old as the nation itself, although the ideology of total abstinence did not become the basis for organized action on a large scale in this country until the early years of the nineteenth century. To early leaders of this movement "temperance" meant moderation rather than total abstinence and the proponents of temperance relied primarily on moral persuasion rather than political action. In the latter half of the century, however, emphasis was increasingly placed on total abstinence and moral persuasion gave way to programs of political action designed to achieve the goal of abstinence by means of state and national prohibition. The prohibitionist movement reached its high-water mark in the passage of the Eighteenth (Prohibition) Amendment in 1919. In spite of the political defeat symbolized by the repeal of national prohibition in the Twenty-first Amendment (1933), the ideology of temperance (abstinence) remains strong.[3]

The persistent strength of the temperance movement in a society characterized by institutionalized drinking for the majority is an interesting contradiction. One still hears occasionally humorous

[1] For a concise but comprehensive survey of the history of drinking in the United States, see McCarthy and Douglass (55, *Ch. 1-5*).

[2] See the summaries of recent studies on drinking in the United States reported in Chapter 2.

[3] For a good historical survey of the temperance movement in America see McCarthy and Douglass (55), especially Chapters 2 and 3; for an analysis of one segment of the temperance movement, see Gusfield (29).

comments about citizens who "stagger to the polls to vote 'dry'" and one legally dry state collects a tax on the sale of alcohol. Margaret Mead (59, *pp. 191 ff.*) has suggested that such persistent straining toward ideal norms which are contradicted by actuality reflects an orientation toward the future and what *might be* which is peculiarly a part of American personality structure.[4] Others have noted both discrepancies between ideal and actual rules of behavior and also the characteristic ways in which such discrepancies are handled. Hollingshead (36), for example, in a discussion of "tabooed pleasures" in a Midwestern town, writes:

"The clandestine pursuit of pleasure is fostered, in opposition to official protestations, by a set of conspiratorial rules which encourage the breaking of taboos by adolescents as well as adults. What we have called the conspiracy of silence . . . represents the central working principles which organize behavior in this area of culture. It may be summarized in the following way: One must not publicly admit the existence of tabooed behavior traits except in condemnatory terms for to recognize their existence is bad, to condone is abhorrent to respectable people and to admit any knowledge of their violation is wicked. Finally, to have any interest in learning about the way the latent patterns work is the worst social error a person can commit. In other words, to violate a taboo is 'bad'; but to talk about it is 'vicious'" (*p. 288*).[5]

Contradictory behavior and attitudes may sometimes be handled by a tacit denial of their existence. However, the psychiatrist Abraham Myerson (65) has emphasized the contradictory attitudes toward and the social ambivalence associated with alcohol use in our society which frequently come to public attention. He traces this ambivalence to the prevalence of two contradictory orientations within the culture, hedonism and asceticism. On the one hand, drinking is an expression of conviviality; it is extolled in song and incorporated in the customs of man as a symbol of good fellowship and social unity. This hedonistic orientation is countered by an equally strong trend toward asceticism in which alcohol is a source of all immorality, the harbinger of degradation and poverty, the enemy of work, duty, religion and sober activity. These orientations are maintained by one or another articulate groups or persons in our society and sometimes by the same groups and persons.

[4] This is a special case of William Graham Sumner's idea of "strain toward consistency" (84, *p. 5*).

[5] See also Myerson (65). An elaboration of the theoretical significance of the "conspiracy of silence" is found in Moore and Tumin (63).

It is appropriate at this point to reemphasize in the consideration of the rules about drinking for teen-agers that the adolescent does not invent the idea of drinking. It is a behavior which young people learn in interaction with adults and, to a lesser extent, with their age peers. The young person must learn whether drinking is appropriate and, if it is, where, when, how, and with whom it is appropriate. In a word, he must learn the shared social rules associated with the use of alcohol.

The opening paragraphs of this chapter suggest that learning the social rules about drinking may be a complicated task in our society. Exposure to contradictory expectations about and ambivalent attitudes toward alcohol use is quite probable. This is so because drinking norms (*1*) are neither always equally prevalent within various groups within the same community (e.g., social groups composed predominantly of Jews, or Catholics, or Mormons) nor equally binding on all members of the same group (e.g., men and women, or adults and adolescents); (*2*) are not tied into a system of obligations to the same degree (e.g., alcohol use may be forbidden, discouraged, permitted or encouraged); (*3*) are not enforced in the same way (e.g., a double standard applied to men and women, or the drunk who behaves himself in contrast to the one who does not).[6] One consequence of this complexity of rules about drinking is the high probability of discrepancy between statements about what one ought to do about alcohol and what may in fact be permitted.[7] Robin Williams (94, *pp. 347 ff.*), for example, has pointed out that in such situations "customary ways of not conforming" or institutionalized variations and evasions of normative patterns are likely to appear. His analysis of institutionalized nonconformity from ideal norms explores the consequences of discrepancy between the transmission of norms in the abstract as a part of the cultural heritage of a group and the application of these norms in specific, concrete social situations. Factors of time, place, values, interests, knowledge and power all complicate the simple conversion of generalized rules ("teen-agers should not drink") into specific behavior appropriate to a given concrete situation ("this 18-year-old teen-ager should not drink at this senior

[6] For a more detailed discussion, see Williams (94, *pp. 25 ff.*) and Stouffer (81).

[7] Linton (51, *pp. 43-54*) has conceptualized this common-sense observation as "ideal" and "actual" and has discussed at some length the implications of the distinction for the analysis of culture.

party").[8] Differences in the perception and the interpretation of appropriate norms are always possible and in some situations probable. Where ambiguities in regard to norms persist, these differences in perception and interpretation may take on the character of "customary ways of not conforming." Williams hypothesizes that such patterns of nonconformity are typically observed in situations in which the deviant behavior (*1*) contributes to the achievement of group goals, (*2*) is practiced by members of the groups against whom social sanctions are difficult to apply, or (*3*) is punished only periodically or ritually insofar as there is insufficient consensus in the community to permit effective prohibition of the behavior.

These hypotheses clearly are useful in understanding the persistence of drinking behavior among some adolescents in spite of the fact that such behavior is characteristically considered deviant both by adults and adolescents themselves as will be shown below. If the ritual uses of alcohol among some ethnic groups are excluded, abstinence is strongly preferred for children in our society. Although there is no systematic evidence on this point, even those parents who permit their children to taste alcoholic beverages when adults are drinking do not permit their children to drink with them. This is reflected in the fact that, in the interviews with students, a number of them referred to tasting alcohol in the presence of parents; none talked of drinking with parents. Such a distinction reflects an awareness on the part of teen-agers who drink that their drinking is peer-group behavior and parents are not peers. Moreover, it is doubtful, although systematic evidence is lacking, that the adult who permits his adolescent offspring to taste alcohol when adults are drinking also makes this distinction so clearly.

Public policy as expressed in law joins parental law in suggesting that drinking by adolescents is deviant behavior. Laws forbidding sale to or the purchase of alcohol by minors are widespread. The intent, if not the letter, of such laws supports the notion that alcohol

[8] A study (85) of the relationship between the moral beliefs of 16-year-old high-school students and their application of these beliefs in specific situational contexts found the correlation low. "The reason lies in the fact that in the life problems several acceptable values were set into conflict with each other. . . ." The conflict of values and the necessity of decision required compromise which was not so obvious when each value could be considered separately. Similarly, Stouffer (81) reports a type of student who has resolved differences in the norms of authority figures and student groups on cheating without apparent difficulty by making situational distinctions and finding common ground between the disparate norms.

use by adolescents should be minimized. In sum, both parental and public law typically support abstinence for the adolescent in principle. Teen-age drinking is deviant behavior in the sense that it is not preferred or encouraged. Yet most such drinking cannot easily be equated with delinquency. There was no indication, for example, that the users in this study considered themselves or were considered by official sanctioning agencies in the community to be delinquents merely because they secured alcohol and drank it in violation of the spirit if not the letter of the law.

In fact, the deviant behavior in this case seemed to be positively valued by the deviants (that is, the users). Drinking appears to have been an important means of self- and social identification for many of them. Drinking was one of the available means of relating themselves to adult status. Moreover, as Williams' hypotheses would lead one to expect, the user was likely to be a person against whom social sanctions were difficult to apply; that is, the older teen-ager who was already playing or soon expecting to play adult roles.

There is an additional peculiarity involved in labeling drinking by adolescents as a deviant act in and of itself. A young person would have to be very unperceptive to miss the point that prohibitions against drinking are age-related. Behavior which is forbidden or discouraged for a 20-year-old suddenly becomes permissible the following year. Furthermore, punishment for speeding up the process of assuming the drinking prerogatives of adulthood is in fact only periodically and ritually applied because there is not sufficient consensus in most communities to permit stringent enforcement of social rules about adolescent drinking, especially when this behavior does not come to the attention of public officials.

What the teen-agers themselves said about the rules governing the use of alcohol by people like themselves illustrates the complexity of rules about teen-age drinking implied in the above paragraphs. Their normative judgments about drinking in terms of the imputed rightness and wrongness of this act and also in terms of the situational factors which qualify these judgments are introduced as cases in point. After a review of the interview materials which give some insight into the normative aspects of teen-age drinking as seen by teen-agers themselves, attention will be given successively to the relationship (*1*) between use and judgments about the rightness and wrongness of use and (*2*) between use and identification with organized religion.

The Norms of Drinking: A Student View

Teen-agers perceived the social rules governing drinking to be very complex. Evidence for this is found in the interviews in which students talked informally, and usually quite frankly, about their experiences with the use of alcohol and their evaluations of those experiences. The following excerpts are illustrative of a commonly encountered point of view:

"I first put down [on the questionnaire] 'drinking is never right,' but I have changed that because I didn't think about it too much at the time. I would say that it's an individual's own business. Well, my girl, for instance, she considers drinking quite bad . . . she won't associate with any people who drink. She considers it bad morals; she thinks everybody gets drunk every time they drink. But I found that not to be—that isn't true. I don't agree with her at all. It's your own business whether you drink or not."

"Well, really, I don't think drinking is right, but I don't know why they do it or why I do it, either. But it's just for fun, I guess; goes along with the party; just to be one of the guys, I guess."

"I circled [on the questionnaire] 'drinking is never right no matter what the circumstances.' [Have you ever tasted alcohol?] Yes, at a Christmas party this year with my relatives. I would rather do it with them. I don't really know why I did it because it didn't enter my mind. I was thirsty and it was cold and I was supposed to be taking a drink to my dad. It was half gone before I got there" [laughs].

"Well, I am very much against drinking. It's alright; I mean, I don't care anything about it. Like people I know, when they have a party, they drink then. I know most of the fathers are this way. They have a beer when the ball game is on or something. I'm not against that at all, but I don't think it is good for their health. I won't mind if my husband drinks but I don't think I will."

"Seeing that I drink myself, I think differently, even though I do drink. I took the last answer, 'drinking is never right no matter what the circumstances'—for teen-agers, that is."

With one exception the students who are quoted here indicated on their questionnaires that they believed drinking to be "wrong." At the same time, both the substance of what they said and the casual way in which they talked about the use of alcohol make it evident that this "wrong" behavior is hedged with a number of conditions. The variety of conditions under which this "wrong" behavior was acceptable to many teen-agers suggests that, for many of them, drinking is better described in terms of situational appropriateness or inappropriateness rather than in terms of rightness or wrongness in an absolute moral sense.

Some teen-agers also explicitly distinguished between moral and pragmatic rationales for abstinence, as the self-identified drinker who said:

"My mother says that I absolutely shouldn't drink; it's immoral. I don't get the deal. She says it's harmful. I believe that, and that's it."

Moreover, pragmatic rationales for abstinence were given by students who variously thought of drinking as "breaking training," too expensive, or as reserved for adults only. For others, drinking was behavior which they could take or leave:

"Well, I don't see that it's a problem in my life. But, I mean, occasionally taking a drink isn't bad as long as you don't go out and get dead drunk and make a fool of yourself."

"I think in general that for kids it doesn't matter so much about drinking. I mean they like to drink, but I don't think they do it just to be smart. A lot of them do, but I don't in general think they drink just to be smart. They drink because they like it. They aren't heavy drinkers. They will drink. They aren't set against it but they aren't all for it."

"Oh, myself, I don't go for drinking at all, but I don't hold it against anybody if they do it properly. You know, social but not make a fool of themselves. There's a few that—they indulge quite a bit, yet they're doing it just for now. I don't think they will turn out to be drunkards."

Some of the students gave "religious reasons" as a basis for abstinence, but there was little indication that the teen-agers generally perceived a close association between participation in organized religion and abstinence. As one said:

"I think drinking is wrong. Quite a few of my friends have religious reasons, believing that it is wrong—I mean, their religion teaches it. And then some of them think it's wrong because they do things that you wouldn't ordinarily do and so that makes it wrong. . . . I know quite a few people, their religion is against it and they drink anyway but I think that most people, if their religion is against it, I don't think they do."

On the other hand, another student reported:

"Our [drinking] group consists of Christian Scientists, a few Catholics, a few Methodists and Jews, but it doesn't make any difference. . . . None of the ministers know us. Only a few of us go to the same church."

Although the relationship between participation in organized religious groups and teen-age drinking will be considered in some detail later in this chapter, it should be emphasized at this point that the perceived relationship is of initial interest. Whether there is a relationship between "religiousness" and abstinence is a question which cannot be resolved on the basis of data analyzed here. In the face of the sacramental use of alcohol in some churches, the toleration of "moderate drinking" by some religious groups and student perceptions that drinking is behavior which is common to a majority of adults at least some of whom are members of religious organizations, it can hardly be argued that identification with organized religion is by definition associated with total abstinence or the evaluation of all drinking as morally wrong.

In fact, some teen-agers were explicit in rejecting the notion that all drinking is illegitimate behavior in American society. Said one:

"In the Army they'll give anybody an alcoholic beverage as long as he is on the post and you can't get drunk. So right there, if alcohol has got anything to hurt you physically, they wouldn't give it to the soldiers."

And another said:

"They don't advertise marijuana so I think that's why most kids are scared to death of it. . . . Alcohol, that's different because they advertise it and everything. Everytime you see it, it looks good and you'll want it."

Some students do perceive that alcohol is available to a segment of the population, the Army, which presumably must be physically fit. Moreover, alcohol is advertised directly and indirectly through mass media of communication. The inference drawn by some students is that such advertising would not exist or would not be condoned if drinking were not legitimate behavior for someone in the society. The acceptance of drinking behavior implicit in such publicity serves to legitimize the desire to drink, quite apart from any influence it may have on creating or intensifying the desire to drink.

The total impression left by the interview data is that drinking, even by teen-agers, is sometimes "right" and sometimes "wrong." A recurrent emphasis of the students was on situational factors related to the appropriateness or inappropriateness of this behavior. Such factors as whether one is a man or woman, an adult or an adolescent, a person who does or does not observe the rules of "moderation" and propriety in where and how much he drinks appear to be important in understanding the normative judgments which teen-agers make about drinking. These factors are as important as abstract notions of the "rightness" or "wrongness" of the behavior which they verbalize. This conclusion is also supported by data from the questionnaire.

The basic proposition about teen-age drinking being developed in these chapters is that what young people think about and do with alcohol reflects their perception of the behavior and attitudes of adults who are important to them. It has been argued that the students in this study correctly perceive that most adults drink at least sometimes; alcohol use is perceived as an integral part of adult social life, particularly when adults are being convivial, celebrating a special event or seeking relief from the tensions of everyday living. Since the achievement of adult status may be assumed to be desired by most adolescents, the probability that a student will be a user and, if a user, will designate himself as a drinker, increases with age and the assumption of adult responsibilities.

The same argument would lead one to expect that the user, who has been shown in fact to be older and more likely to be involved in playing adult roles than others, would also be more likely than the nonuser to express approval of some drinking for some teen-agers. Similarly, among users, the self-designated drinker would be more likely than the nondrinker to express approval. The distribution of responses to a question about the approval or disapproval of drinking by teen-agers "your own age" is consistent with these expectations (Table 20).

A minority of the nonusers (36%), in contrast to 73% of the users, thought that some drinking is "all right" for those their own age. For example, among self-designated drinkers, 81% of the boys and 92% of the girls expressed approval of some drinking by their teen-age peers; among the self-designated nondrinkers, 63% of the boys and 71% of the girls made this judgment.

The data in Table 20 also invite several additional observations. First, unqualified approval or disapproval of drinking by these teen-agers was the exception rather than the rule. Among nonusers, for instance, only 17% of the boys who considered drinking wrong (58%) considered it wrong without qualification in contrast to the 41% who considered it wrong but "one's own business" (31%), or wrong "except to try it once" (10%). Similarly, while 22% of the girl nonusers considered teen-age drinking always wrong, 34% con-

TABLE 20.—*Responses to, "Which of the Following Best Describes Your Personal Opinion about Drinking By People Your Own Age?" By Use, Self-Designation and Sex, in Per Cent*

	Nonusers		*Users*			
			Nondrinkers		Drinkers	
Opinion	*Boys*	*Girls*	*Boys*	*Girls*	*Boys*	*Girls*
Drinking is all right	*36*	*36*	*63*	*71*	*81*	*92*
Unconditional	2	1	1	0	8	2
If parents approve, supervise	7	10	17	34	7	10
Other conditions	27	25	45	37	66	80
Drinking is wrong	*58*	*60*	*33*	*24*	*16*	*8*
Unconditional	17	22	6	8	5	0
Except to try it once	10	4	3	2	2	2
It's one's own business	31	34	24	14	9	6
No answer	6	4	4	5	3	0
Totals	*100*	*100*	*100*	*100*	*100*	*100*
N	104	161	172	107	129	48

sidered such drinking "one's own business" and an additional 4% considered it wrong "except to try it once."

On the other hand, the users did not characteristically give unqualified approval to drinking by their age peers. Among the nondrinkers only 1% of the boys and no girls gave unconditional approval to drinking while among the drinkers only 8% of the boys and 2% of the girls made this response.

A second point suggested by these data is the relatively larger proportion of self-designated nondrinkers among the users who approved of drinking by their age peers "if with parent's approval or if drinking is properly supervised." Seventeen per cent of the boy and 34% of the girl nondrinkers qualified their approval in this way. This is consistent with the argument advanced earlier that the user designating himself as a nondrinker is more likely than the nonuser but less likely than the user who designates himself as a drinker to be identified with adult role playing. For the user who thinks of himself as a nondrinker, the large residue of his subordinate status as an adolescent is reflected in his dependence on adult approval and supervision. He, more than other users, plays at rather than plays the drinking role associated with adult status.

Third, a small proportion of the users indicate that "drinking is never right" for people their age. It has already been noted that in the interviews with students, some who made this response wanted to qualify it, particularly to indicate that their assessment was confined only to people their own age. But, the interview materials also suggest that some users were quite ambivalent about their drinking. It appeared that some of them viewed drinking as morally wrong but socially expedient or necessary. Although special attention has not been given to these students, their ambivalence and its possible association with peculiarities in their drinking behavior poses a question for further research.

Such indications of ambivalence about drinking as these were not peculiarly concentrated among the nondrinkers. This is another indication that the choice of the label nondrinker among users reflects a teen-ager's notion of how far along in the transition he is between adolescence and adulthood. This self-designation is not in itself an indication of ambivalence about the rightness of drinking behavior.

A fourth observation based on the data presented in Table 20 is suggested when the distribution of approval and disapproval of drinking among teen-agers found in the sample of nonusers is taken as an estimate of the distribution which would be found among all nonusers among students in the study. This procedure permits an estimate of the proportion of all students who approve and disapprove of drinking among these teen-agers. It also gives some idea about the relationships between approval–disapproval and sex, use and self-designation as drinker or nondrinker. An estimated 50% of all boys and 44% of all girls in the eleventh and twelfth grades of the schools studied would be expected to express at least conditional approval of some drinking by teen-agers. Among approving (drinking is all right) students, half of the boys and 73% of the girls would be nonusers. Among the remaining 50% of the boys and 56% of the girls who disapprove of drinking by persons their own age, only 13% of the boys and 20% of the girls would disapprove unconditionally.

Thus, in a state that attempts to restrict alcohol consumption by minors through restrictive legislation and through temperance education, but in a community in which teen-agers perceive most adults to use alcohol at least sometimes, one would expect to find some ambivalence toward drinking among teen-agers. Some ambivalence was in evidence in the interviews; ambiguity was also reflected in the rather even split between those teen-agers who considered some drinking by people their own age "all right" and those who considered it "wrong." Further evidence was found in the observation that approval and disapproval were characteristically conditional. The proportion of teen-agers who approved of some use by persons their own age was also considerably greater than the proportion who were users.

These data bring into focus once again the transitional status of the adolescent. Characteristically he perceived some drinking to be an integral part of adult social life but not an integral part of teen-age social life. Most of these young people reported themselves to be abstinent at the time of this study. A significant minority will continue the abstinence of the teen years into and through adulthood. But for the minority who are already drinking and for the majority who sooner or later probably will, there is the problem of resolving the ambiguities of laws which forbid the purchase of alcohol until age 21 but which are less clear about the conditions under which use is permitted. There is a problem of resolving the ambiguities suggested by formal and informal education about the evils of alcohol or the virtues of temperance in a community in which most adults are perceived as users.

The potential adolescent user of alcohol is faced with a problem of timing his behavior in such a way as to minimize the conflict between his own developing notions of self as an adult and adult notions about when he has "come of age." A major part of his problem is solved in time by the legal termination of his status as a minor. Before this time a minority of teen-agers, a minority whose size increases with the age of the teen-agers involved, participate in drinking behavior, in spite of the fact that it is considered deviant by many of the adult authority figures in the adolescent's life.

A majority of the students in this study evaluated drinking by persons their age as "wrong." Yet it is apparent that many of their age peers have developed what Williams (94) has called "customary ways of not conforming" to this expectation. Over one third of the nonusers consider this behavior "all right" and almost another third believe that it is wrong "but one's own business." Williams has also specified why one would expect these developments. In the first place, the deviant behavior, drinking in this case, can contribute to the achievement of an important goal in the life of an adolescent; drinking can be a symbolic means of dissolving the adolescent status and identifying the user with the life style of adults who are perceived to use alcohol in a wide variety of social situations. Second, it is difficult to apply sanctions against use in a community in which a majority of adults are presumably correctly perceived to drink themselves, especially when the adolescent drinker is older and playing, or on the verge of playing, adult roles associated with marriage, entrance into the armed forces or a full-time job. Third, punishment of the deviation is only sporadically and ritually enforced within a community in which, by inference, there is insufficient consensus to permit effective prohibition of the behavior. The indication of exposure to personal use of alcohol in the home by many of the adolescent users illustrates this last point.

Drinking Behavior and Organized Religion

The ambiguities which surround the rules about drinking for adolescents in our society can also be illustrated by analyzing the relationship between identification with organized religion by an adolescent and his drinking behavior. Two of the important functions of organized religious groups are to define the content of a supernaturally sanctioned ethic and to inculcate among its members both an awareness of this ethic and a commitment to it. With regard to the ethical implications of alcohol use, the principal religious faiths in our society agree in condemning drunkenness. They are not in agreement, however, about the compatibility of drinking which does not result in inebriety with religious principles.[9] Congregations of Jews, Catholics and some Protestants use alcohol sacramentally and do not condemn all other uses of alcohol as inherently wrong. A majority of Protestants, and therefore a majority of persons identified with organized religion in the United States, nevertheless belong to religious organizations which historically have either condemned all drinking as morally indefensible or at least have looked on it as behavior which should be discouraged. There is some evidence indicating that members of Protestant denominations which condemn drinking as morally wrong are in fact less likely than others to use alcohol; yet the same studies have indicated that, even in such denominations, a majority of the adherents may be users.[10]

[9] For a summary of pronouncements of various religious organizations, see Bainton (3).

[10] For example, Skolnick (76) argues that different religious group attitudes lead to different kinds of drinking behavior. However, using the sample of college

Unfortunately, in the public school context in which this research was carried out, identification of the students by religious preference was not permitted by school officials. Therefore, it is not possible to describe the distribution of users and self-identified drinkers by religious preference. It is nevertheless possible to explore alcohol use among these high-school students in terms (*1*) of their reported participation in organized religious activities and (*2*) of their assessment of parental interest in religious activities. Admittedly, the quality of an individual's religious life cannot be determined by asking him questions about the number of times he participates in organized religious activities or by asking him to assess his parents' interest in such activities. These gross measures, however, can provide some insight into the relationship between alcohol use by teen-agers in a given community and (*1*) exposure to religious organizations and (*2*) differences in perceived family interest in religious activities.

Among these students, a positive relationship was found between reported monthly attendance at organized religious activities and the probability of being a nonuser (Table 21). Among boys, for example, 12% of the nonusers, in contrast to 16% of the nondrinkers and 22% of the drinkers, reported no monthly church attendance. At the other extreme, 22% of the boy nonusers reported attending religious activities five or more times in the average month as compared with about 10% of the users.

The girls in the study may be similarly described. Seven per cent of the nonusers, 7% of the nondrinkers, but 15% of the drinkers re-

TABLE 21.—*Average Monthly Church Attendance By Use, Self-Designation and Sex, in Per Cent*

	Nonusers		*Users*			
			Nondrinkers		Drinkers	
Attendance	*Boys*	*Girls*	*Boys*	*Girls*	*Boys*	*Girls*
None	12	7	16	7	22	15
One or two times	17	17	31	33	23	13
Three or four times	43	43	32	43	36	44
Five or more times	22	30	9	13	10	22
No answer	6	3	12	4	9	6
Totals	*100*	*100*	*100*	*100*	*100*	*100*
N	104	161	172	107	129	48

students developed by Straus and Bacon, Skolnick found that 70% of the Methodist and Baptist students, although identified with churches historically committed to abstinence, used beverage alcohol.

ported no attendance in the average month. At the other extreme, 30% of the girl nonusers reported attending religious activities five or more times in the average month, in contrast to 13% of the nondrinkers and 22% of the drinkers.

The association between religious participation and the probability of being a nonuser can be illustrated in another way. If the sample distribution of reported activity among the sample of nonusers is used as an estimate of the distribution of this characteristic among all nonusers in this study, it is found that as reported participation increases the proportion of users decreases. Among boys who reported no attendance, for example, 56% were nonusers, while 66% of those who reported some participation (one to four times a month) and 83% of those who reported extensive participation (five or more times a month) were nonusers.

Similarly, among girls, 42% of those who reported no participation were nonusers in contrast to 78% of those reporting some participation and 91% of those who participated five or more times in the average month.

Analysis of the relationship between assessment of parental interest in religious activity and use of alcohol gives additional support to the observation that, among these teen-agers, exposure to a home environment in which religious interest is high increases the probability that an individual will be a nonuser (Table 22). Among boys, for example, 50% of the nonusers assessed parental interest in religious activities to be "high" or "very high." Among boy users, on the other hand, 30% of the self-designated nondrinkers and 34% of the drinkers made this assessment.

Among girls, a similar relationship was observed. Forty-six per

TABLE 22.—*Student Assessment of Parental Family's Interest in Religious Activities, By Use, Self-Designation and Sex, in Per Cent*

	Nonusers		*Users*			
			Nondrinkers		Drinkers	
Family Interest	*Boys*	*Girls*	*Boys*	*Girls*	*Boys*	*Girls*
None	4	2	4	3	3	8
Very little	9	13	9	8	11	21
Some	35	39	50	55	49	32
High	40	31	24	26	26	29
Very high	10	15	6	8	8	10
No answer	2	0	7	0	3	0
Totals	*100*	*100*	*100*	*100*	*100*	*100*
N	104	161	172	107	129	48

cent of the nonusers considered parental interest in religious activities to be "high" or "very high" in contrast to 34% of the nondrinkers and 39% of the drinkers.

Again, the positive association between perceived interest of the parental family in religious activities and the probability of being a nonuser can be illustrated by noting the distribution of users and nonusers among students who assessed parental interest high (i.e., "high" or "very high") as compared with those who assessed this interest as low (i.e., "some," "very little," or "none"). Among boys who assessed parental interest as high, 76% were nonusers, while among those assessing low parental interest, 60% were nonusers. Similarly, among girls, of the students assessing parental interest to be high, 88% were nonusers as compared with 83% of those who reported parental religious interest to be low.

It is apparent from these analyses that, while religious participation and exposure to a parental environment in which religious interest is high were associated with abstinence among these students, other factors are contributory. This is indicated by the fact that nonusers are as numerous as users even among those teenagers who report least activity and least parental interest. On the other hand, extensive participation and high parental interest in religious activities does not insure that a teen-ager will be abstinent.

One would not expect this to be the case if the particular religious tradition to which the teen-ager is exposed is permissive toward some use of alcohol. As indicated previously, the inability to secure information about religious affiliation from the students under investigation does not permit resolution of this question. On the basis of other research findings, however, one would hypothesize that users who indicate extensive participation, high parental interest, or both, would be affiliated with a religious tradition which does not consider all drinking to be immoral. But it would be further hypothesized that, even for teen-agers exposed to a religious tradition permitting some social uses of alcohol, use among teen-agers so exposed would still reflect factors of age and sex.

Teen-Age Drinking and the Law

A brief comment on the relationship between drinking and the law is appropriate before the discussion of teen-age rules is terminated. In the state in which the study was made, the sale of alcoholic beverages to persons under 21 years is prohibited by law.

Although the question of the legality of drinking was not covered in the questionnaire, the interview data left no doubt that the students were aware that their drinking was illegal. They were aware, for example, that an identification card is needed to purchase alcohol legally and were equally aware that being caught drinking or in the possession of alcohol by the police meant trouble for themselves and their parents. The behavior of the majority was consistent with the law. This fact is not in itself a demonstration that the observed abstinence is explained to an important degree by the legal rules intended to minimize drinking among adolescents.

There was no indication in the interviews, for example, that the awareness of the illegality of their use of alcohol was a major deterrent to drinking among users, although it apparently emphasized to them the need for caution. The availability of alcohol in the home, at the corner grocery or through the buying services of a friend of legal age made it possible "for anyone who wants it to get it." Furthermore, typical descriptions of teen-age drinking parties did not emphasize that precautions were taken in fear of an imminent threat of detection by police. And even when detection was considered as a possibility, there was little indication that dire consequences were expected to follow.

There was also a striking absence of expressions indicating that the teen-ager who drank considered himself as a "law-breaker," much less a "delinquent." This finding is congruent with the observation that the students emphasized the situational appropriateness or inappropriateness rather than the morality or immorality of drinking. It is quite possible, though undemonstrated, that legal restraints have an effect on where, when, what, how and with whom adolescents drink. It is less apparent that such rules have any effect on whether an adolescent with the characteristics of the user in this study will drink if the significant adult figures in his environment themselves drink.

Conclusions

Most of the teen-agers in this study expressed disapproval of drinking by individuals of their own age. Their disapproval is consistent both with their reported abstinence and with their perception that individuals like themselves are in the majority.

This characterization, while essentially true, oversimplifies the complexity of social rules surrounding the use of alcohol in our society, particularly surrounding use by adolescents. An adolescent in almost any community in the United States is likely to be exposed to two contradictory cultural traditions about alcohol use. Moreover, even if he is exposed to a tradition which permits some alcohol use by adults, he is almost certain to be exposed to social rules in the form of parental or public law which imply the desirability of deferring drinking behavior until he is adult. Also the rules apply somewhat differently to boys and girls.

What these young people said about the rightness and wrongness of drinking by their age peers reflects these complexities. A strong preference for qualified judgments about drinking was evident; the qualifications sometimes referred to age, sometimes to sex, sometimes to situation. But for all their qualifications, considerably more of these students expressed approval of drinking by their age peers than in fact reported drinking at the time of the study, as though anticipating their own behavior later.

The strong preference for qualified judgments about alcohol use suggests that these young people did not perceive the abstinence of adolescents as necessarily total and permanent. The association observed between abstinence and identification with organized religion does not constitute crucial contrary evidence. This association may reflect differences in the moral assessment of alcohol use by various religious groups; in this case, for example, abstinence and high religious identification may reflect the fact that most students with such religious interest have inherited a tradition of abstinence. The minority of users with high religious interest would simply reflect a different tradition. The absence of information about the religious preferences of these students makes the resolution of this question impossible. But an equally plausible line of investigation for future research might be the association between religious organizations and what might be called conventional morality. Conventional morality in the sense in which it is used here might be illustrated by the acceptance of a double standard of behavior for men and women or by emphasis on the subordination of children to their parents. Since organized religious groups are typically controlled by adults, adolescents who are most active in and who report high parental interest in such organizations might be expected to conform to adult definitions of appropriate behavior for adolescents. There is little question that one of these expectations is that drinking by adolescents is generally inappropriate, whatever the appropriateness of this behavior for the adult.

Finally, investigation of the rules of drinking for teen-agers gives additional support to the basic proposition being developed in these chapters. Users, who are older and more likely than others to be playing adult roles, are more likely than nonusers to approve of drinking by individuals of their own age. Many nonusers seem to anticipate their own drinking behavior later by indicating that, under certain circumstances, drinking by teen-agers is "all right."

Chapter 5

WHY PEOPLE DRINK: A TEEN-AGE VERSION

THE ASSESSMENT of human motivation is difficult. People do not always know why they behave as they do. Even if they know, or think they do, they are not necessarily willing to give this information to someone else or capable of doing so. Nevertheless, the question, "Why did you do that?" is perennial. All of us not only ask the question continually; we also expect and usually get an answer.

The answers we get do not tell us everything we want to know about motives for human behavior. But we can learn something from the answers we get, for example, to a question like, "Why do adults drink?" or "Why do you drink?" At a minimum we may get some insight about what drinking means to an adolescent and what he assumes it means to others. We can learn something about how certain types of meaning are shared by teen-agers. Understanding what drinking means to them in turn helps us to interpret why most adolescents at one time or another experiment with the use of alcohol and some of them come to integrate its use with their characteristic way of relating themselves to the environment.

Reporting and interpreting a teen-age version of why adults and adolescents drink is the task of this chapter. Before their responses are reported, however, it is appropriate to suggest a way of thinking about and looking at what these responses may tell us about motives for drinking.

A Situational Approach to the Problem

There is increasing consensus among social psychologists that human motivation, that is, the mobilization and selective direction of energy, is best understood in a social context. Simply stated, the assumptions of this way of looking at human motives are these: (*1*) Any item in social behavior is understood only as it is seen as part of a social situation; (*2*) in social interaction, a person not only develops responses assumed to be appropriate in that situation but also incorporates the response patterns of others into his predisposition to react in similar situations in the future; (3) therefore, attention must be given to the social context in which interaction occurs as well as to the individuals acting in it (14, 15).

More or less stable patterns of behavior for both self and others are developed in repeated social interaction. For this reason, neither the process of identifying an appropriate course of action nor predispositions to act in a predictable fashion can be studied apart from an individual's definition of the particular situation in which he is acting at some point in time. Fundamental aspects of this situational definition include an individual's conception of himself and the symbols by which he is recognized and with which he is identified.

A shared system of symbols is the keystone of the social interaction process. In symbols, Ernst Cassirer (10) has observed:

"Man has, as it were, discovered a new method of adapting himself or his environment. Between the receptor system and the effector system, which are found in all animal species, we find in man a third link which we may describe as the symbolic system. This new acquisition transforms the whole of human life. As compared with other animals, man lives not merely in a broader reality, he lives, so to speak, in a new dimension of reality" (*pp. 42-43*).

The importance of this symbolic transformation of stimuli for the analysis and understanding of human behavior has been increasingly recognized by behavioral scientists. While it is impractical for our purposes to document in detail the intellectual history of this idea and to assess its impact on theories of human behavior, it is relevant to indicate briefly some contributions to an understanding of symbolism made by anthropologists, social psychologists and sociologists. In turn, these ideas may be shown to be directly related to an understanding of motivation, and specifically, motivation to drink or to abstain among adolescents.

Symbolism and Motivation

Language being a principal mechanism for the transmission of culture, this class of symbols has attracted attention as an area of anthropological interest. But language is not merely a vehicle for culture transmission. A. I. Hallowell (31) has made the point succinctly:

"Man's psychological responses to physical objects of his external environment can only be understood in terms of the *traditional* meanings which these latter have for him. He never views the outer world freshly or responds to his fellows entirely free from the influence which these meanings exert on his thought and conduct. . . . Man's attitude toward them is a function of reality culturally defined, not in terms of their mere physical existence. . . . Consequently, the objects of the external world, as meaningfully defined in a traditional ideology, constitute the reality to which individuals habituated to a particular system of beliefs actually respond."[1]

This means that the response to natural objects or persons is influenced by shared beliefs about what these objects do to and for persons. An individual's symbolic transformation of the world of his experience, then, is not random but is integrally related to a system of traditional meanings which structure and limit, if not determine, his perception of the world about him.[2]

The implications of this common symbolic transformation of experiences have also been explored in the field of psychology, particularly by perception theorists (8, 75). Among these theorists, there appears to be essential agreement that the most important adjustments of the individual are not a consequence of the direct effect of stimuli on the human organism. Rather, behavior is governed by learned responses to stimuli based on previous experience with the stimuli or, in lieu of experience with the particular stimuli, with culture patterns which suggest a course of action. The traditional meaning imputed to a wide range of stimuli facilitates their recognition and placement in an understandable scheme because such placement suggests an appropriate behavioral response.

But more important from the standpoint of our particular interest in motives for drinking, one also learns in the social interaction the emotional significance which certain persons or objects should have for the perceiver and his conception of self. A striking illustration of the affective dimension of symbols is found in Lindesmith's analysis of opiate addiction. The user of opiates, says Lindesmith (50),

"acquires the customs and attitudes which other users impart to him. . . . He applies to his own conduct the generalized symbols which the

[1] For a development of this idea in an available source, see Hallowell (32).

[2] Hallowell's statement summarizes in essence one of the important implications of the Sapir–Whorf hypothesis relating language to behavior. For example, see Sapir (73); also Whorf (93). For a brief summary and critical review of the Sapir–Whorf hypothesis, see Hoijer (35).

group applies to it; this means that the drug user assimilates the attitudes and sentiments which are current in his social milieu. . . . Thus [addiction] presupposes the individual's membership in social groups, and his ability to communicate with his fellows in terms of language symbols. . . . It depends on those complex functions which are made possible only by the symbolic structure of language" (*p. 89*).

"It is through the use of the social symbols of language in conversation with himself and with others that the personality changes involved in becoming an addict are initiated and carried out. The individual, when he uses the symbols which society provides him also assumes the attitudes appropriate to those symbols when he applies them to himself" (*p. 166*).

This extreme example makes an important point. Symbols whose traditional meanings are learned in social interaction come to have affective, motivational, and normative as well as cognitive connotations.[3] That is, alcohol may be variously perceived as a chemical, a drug or a beverage. Its use may be important or unimportant, approved or disapproved behavior for any given individual. But in any event, what alcohol means is a matter of learning.

C. Wright Mills (62) has emphasized another facet of the motivational connotations built into symbols. He asserts that "motives are words" not denoting anything in individuals but rather denoting anticipated responses to the question "Why did you do that?" Therefore, out of social interaction arise "vocabularies of motives" which provide socially acceptable answers to such a question; the shared answers become traditional. It is for this reason that motives may be imputed by others even before they are admitted by the self. In Lindesmith's phrase, one "applies to his own conduct the generalized symbols which the group applies to it."

A similar approach to the problem of motivation, but one which goes a step further, has been suggested by Nelson Foote (26). Motivated behavior is characterized by its future orientation and by the selection and control of alternative means to ends. When an actor defines a situation as calling for a particular act with more or less anticipated consequence, he then releases energy appropriate for performing that act. Mobilization of energy, Foote asserts, always follows after, never precedes, definition of situations which call for particular acts.

Foote probably overstates his case and, implicitly, overrationalizes human behavior. However, his basic point is well taken. The key to

[3] For an extended discussion of this point, see Parsons (68).

the understanding of the mobilization and expenditure of energy is found in the process of identification; that is, in the investment of objects in social situations with significance for the self.[4]

The Process of Identification and Response to Beverage Alcohol

Granting that understanding symbolism and the process of identification is fundamental to understanding motivation, one is still confronted with the practical problem of understanding why an individual comes to attach importance to some persons, objects or self-concepts rather than others. Why, for example, should alcohol be used by some persons and avoided by others? Why should some persons who use alcohol prefer to think of themselves as drinkers, others as nondrinkers. Both these questions reflect a problem that has persistently presented itself to those attempting to understand why, in situations where alternative courses of behavior are possible, a particular mode of behavior is selected.

A proposed answer to the problem which appears promising for the study of teen-age drinking is that of Eisenstadt (19). Eisenstadt, following the lead of Robert Merton, suggests that choice among alternative courses of behavior is related both to the status and status aspirations of the individual and also to the patterns of the institutionalized behavior in a society. That is, choice is related to shared definitions of the self-concept one ought to desire, the status–conferral possibilities of certain self-concepts as compared with others, and a projection of future status aspirations.

The evidence presented in Chapter 3 should be recalled at this point. It has been noted that teen-agers in this study perceive most adults as drinkers. Moreover, particularly among boys, the teenager who plays or prefers to play adult roles is more likely than others both to use alcohol and to identify himself as a drinker. This suggests that an important aspect of the drinking behavior of the high-school student is the status-conferral possibilities of the act of drinking where the society makes adulthood a valued status and institutionalizes drinking as one aspect of what it means to be an adult.

[4] A similar theoretical analysis of motivation is found in Becker and Carper (6): ". . . individuals identify themselves—answer the question 'Who am I?'—in terms of the names and categories current in the groups in which they participate. By applying these labels to themselves, they learn who they are and how they ought to behave, acquire a self and a set of perspectives in terms of which their conduct is shaped."

Additional insight into what drinking means to the teen-ager and the status–conferral possibilities of this act is evident in the shared "vocabulary of motives" verbalized by students. That is, there is a conventional set of responses in anticipation of the question, "Why do adults and high-school students drink?" about which teen-agers are in essential agreement. In articulating this "vocabulary" students suggest what they perceive to be the meaning of this behavior both for themselves and others and for the social groups in which they are or expect to be members.

One final point remains to be considered before we turn to the analysis of the data on motivation for drinking among the teen-agers in this study. Most of the literature on the use of alcohol in American society has tended to concentrate on the dysfunctional aspects of this behavior for both the individual and the society. This point was documented in some detail in Chapter 2. One consequence of this emphasis has been that drinking has frequently been approached as though its use could only be dysfunctional because personal and social problems follow its use for a minority of users. On the contrary, cumulative evidence clearly indicates that alcoholic beverages are considered as something to be enjoyed by many people and that their pleasure-giving values are perceived as more than counterbalancing any unpleasant features.[5]

The unfortunate consequences of some uses of alcohol are obvious. But it is equally obvious, in the face of the literature which has been reviewed previously, that some uses of alcohol are perceived to do something for as well as to individuals and social groups. This is the proposition to be developed in the paragraphs which follow.

What Drinking Means to Adults and Teen-Agers: Some Comments by Teen-Agers

A "Vocabulary of Motives" for Adult Drinking

When the teen-agers in this study were asked, "What are the three most important reasons adults drink?" three themes were apparent in their answers (Table 23). The first theme focuses on identification with social groups and sociability. When adults are "partying" or being convivial, the situation is defined as likely to involve drinking. As one teen-age girl phrased it:

[5] On this point, see Lemert (49).

TABLE 23.—*Responses to "What Are the Three Most Important Reasons Adults Drink?" By Use, Self-Designation and Sex, in Per Cent**

	Nonusers		Users			
			Nondrinkers		Drinkers	
Reasons	*Boys*	*Girls*	*Boys*	*Girls*	*Boys*	*Girls*
1. Sociability						
to be sociable, one of the group	10	18	18	14	18	21
to avoid being left out, considered different	3	2	2	2	1	1
to celebrate a special occasion	10	8	9	9	11	9
to continue a family style, a matter of habit	15	5	5	4	7	7
2. Self-expression						
pleasurable relaxation	8	10	13	14	19	15
to enhance conception of self as smart, grownup	7	4	3	2	2	1
3. Anxiety reduction, relief from family, financial, personal problems	17	38	21	29	25	43
4. Other						
miscellaneous	14	4	6	11	5	2
incomplete responses	16	11	23	15	12	1
Totals	*100*	*100*	*100*	*100*	*100*	*100*

* Multiple responses are included in all totals. The number of responses of a given kind is expressed as a percentage of the total number of responses.

"Maybe people like drinking. I mean, lots of people do. And if you go to a party and everybody else is drinking and you sit in the corner—I mean, naturally if you [the interviewer] went with a bunch of men, you'd know yourself that if you didn't drink you would feel out of place. I think this is primarily the reason."

The implication is that, if one is not drinking when others are, one is not "partying" and hence is not a full-fledged member of the group. Similar comments were made in many of the interviews. Furthermore, drinking among adults was associated by these students with perpetuating out of habit a form of behavior associated with important social groups with which they are identified and with the celebration of holidays or special events. In these various contexts emphasis is on alcohol as a social beverage.

A second theme was that of self-expression or fulfillment. Students repeatedly referred to the pleasurable effects associated with drinking. One "floats on air," is "high," gets "in a real happy mood," gets "thrills" or "oomph." Or perhaps drinking is simply "refreshing":

"Well, I don't like drinking myself very well, but some people consider it refreshing and they take it just—they don't drink heavily but they just take it for refreshment. I don't think that is bad, but if they go too far with it, well, I don't like that at all."

Another facet of this theme is the possibility of saying something about oneself that one wants said. One can "drink like a man" or appear "smart" or "grown-up" when drinking.

The third theme is anxiety or tension reduction. Here alcohol is viewed as a convenient tranquilizer for adults who have family, financial or social problems. One student managed to touch on all three of the common themes:

"There's the first kind of person who drinks to be sociable. And there's another that drinks—well, because his friends drink. Some people drink because they don't have friends or anything and they are really what you call an outsider. So they drink and become an alcoholic. Then some people drink on occasions to celebrate and some drink to be sociable."

Not many students associated drinking to relieve tension with alcoholism in such an unqualified fashion as this student. But the emphasis on drinking in response to tension and anxiety was common.

Among boys, the sociability theme appeared most often; anxiety reduction was second; and self-fulfillment third. Among girls, the anxiety reduction theme was first; sociability was a close second; and self-fulfillment was third. It should be noted that, in spite of the fact that anxiety reduction is mentioned with interesting frequency by all these students, sociability and self-expression as reasons for drinking by adults nevertheless account for approximately half of the responses.

A "Vocabulary of Motives" for Teen-Age Drinking

When teen-agers assessed the reasons why people like themselves drink, the sociability and self-fulfillment themes used to describe reasons for adult drinking were again apparent. But the anxiety reduction theme was strikingly absent (Table 24). One of the students summed it up this way:

"I don't think teen-agers drink because they are blue or anything, like maybe some grownups do, feeling sorry for themselves. I don't think

TABLE 24.—*Responses to "What Are the Three Most Important Reasons Teen-Agers in High School Drink?" By Use, Self-Designation and Sex, in Per Cent**

	Nonusers		*Users*			
			Nondrinkers		Drinkers	
Reasons	*Boys*	*Girls*	*Boys*	*Girls*	*Boys*	*Girls*
1. Sociability						
to be sociable, one of the group	11	15	11	11	15	19
to avoid being left out, considered different	16	21	14	17	15	19
to celebrate a special occasion	2	0	1	1	4	1
to continue a family style, a matter of habit	4	2	2	2	3	2
2. Self-expression						
pleasurable relaxation	2	1	2	2	7	3
to enhance conception of self as smart, grownup	41	41	34	43	32	38
3. Anxiety reduction, relief from family, financial, personal problems	1	2	2	3	3	2
4. Other						
miscellaneous	8	7	8	5	9	11
incomplete responses	15	11	26	16	12	5
Totals	*100*	*100*	*100*	*100*	*100*	*100*

* Multiple responses are included in all totals. The number of responses of a given kind is expressed as a percentage of the total number of responses.

teen-agers drink for that reason. But I have been around quite a few people that have drunk and I know that they either drink to be sociable or either they drink because they want to show off and be smart and show others how much they can drink. And these are the only reasons I can think of why people drink except maybe that they like it."

The accuracy of his observation is suggested by the fact that approximately three-fourths of all responses to the question, "What are the three most important reasons teen-agers in high school drink?" emphasized either sociability or self-fulfillment. Material from the interviews particularly helps to elaborate what drinking means to adolescents in high school.

Drinking and Status Transformation

"Being smart" apparently implied for these students the premature playing of adult roles. Teen-age drinking calls attention to itself in large part because it is unusual behavior, behavior ordinarily appropriate for adults:

"I've talked quite a bit about 'drinking' in the last couple of weeks because of all the senior parties. You can notice it more that way. A teen-ager goes out and it doesn't matter how much he drinks. If they drink a lot, that's different because they will get in trouble. But even if they drink just one bottle or one drink, most of them just start acting smart and . . . just to show off. That's the way I see it; they put it on just to show-off."

"Being smart" as a reason for drinking by teen-agers was frequently mentioned and often associated with "proving [one] can hold it." Presumably what one proves is more than the fact that one "can hold it" in a literal sense. What one is attempting to convey to his peers by means of drinking is "Look, I am drinking like an adult [or man]." That is, in attempting to "act grown-up" teen-agers frequently "act smart" and attempt to prove they "can hold it." This interpretation makes sense in the light of the teen-ager's aspirations to become an adult coupled with his perception of the adult as a person likely to drink. It is equally interesting that the students were aware that drinking may be histrionic, that the effects of drinking may be faked and deliberately exaggerated.[6]

Still another facet of the use of alcohol to transform the adolescent's status is suggested by the repeated reference in the interviews to "coming of age." This phrase means in part that one has attained the legal age for drinking:

"Some people think you should drink on your twenty-first birthday. Why? Because they come of age. . . . They want to take some right then because they know they have come of age and can get the stuff better than when they were underage."

But more than this, "coming of age" is implicitly equated with the playing of adult roles; such roles, for example, as a holder of a full-time job, the married person or a member of the armed services. All of these roles may be played prior to the attainment of the age of legal adulthood. Since the majority of students expect to assume one or more of these essentially adult roles shortly after graduation from high school, if not before, the observations (*1*) that the pro-

[6] Lemert (49) refers to these particular status-conferral potentialities of drinking among the Northwest Coast Indians. Antonio Arce, a sociologist and native of Costa Rica, has described in personal conversations how drinkers in Costa Rica frequently refer to each other as "muy hombre" (very much a man) when drinking.

portion of *users* tends to increase with the age of the students and (2) that the probability of drinking is at its maximum during the activities which end the senior year in high school take on new meaning:

"Well, I don't know how to explain it, but especially the fellows in the senior year and especially these last few months, practically all the fellows have been drinking. Not all to excess but all drinking quite a bit. After they get out of high school the fellows straighten up again and within a few months after graduation they are the same people you have always known."

"Oh, we usually drink when my friends come along or something like that. Maybe on some special occasions; not every weekend but like during Senior Night, our senior activities."

Drinking as it is described here appears to be an improvised rite of passage between adolescence and adulthood.

A similar observation may be made about the implications of entrance into the armed forces, which a number of students also associated with drinking. Going into the armed services implies the achievement of adult status insofar as effective parental control is severed and some measure of financial and emotional independence is expected:

"My friend wanted to have a party for the fellows in our class who are going into the army, see—the Marines. So we have a party and, of course, alcohol—beer and stuff was brought."

Although all teen-age drinking cannot be explained altogether by its status potentialities, much of it can be. Alcohol serves as an institutionalized way of symbolizing the dissolution of adolescence and the transformation of the individual into a new position in the social group. This conclusion implies that drinking does something for some teen-agers that they want done. Drinking is important for validating their self-conceptions as adults or their claims to adult status. It might be argued that behavior which is desirable by the user and his peers is undesirable from the point of view of persons in other groups in which these teen-agers also participate. Without question, many adults as well as many teen-agers view the drinking of the high-school student as undesirable. Drinking by adolescents invades the prerogatives of the adult and may, in some circumstances, result in additional restraints being placed on the behavior of nonusers. Such drinking frequently may involve illegal acts other than the purchase and use of alcoholic beverages by minors. Nevertheless, it may be argued that in a society in which some drinking is institutionalized for adults and which has only a minimum number of institutionalized rites of passage between childhood and adulthood, drinking serves a purpose. Drinking may contribute in such a situation to the validation of the self-conception of some teen-agers who claim adult status and, to this extent, contribute to the integration of these teen-agers into the larger adult society. That some other means of integration might be preferred, and especially by some groups in the society, is another issue.

Peer Group Identification

Both adults and adolescents are said to drink in order "to be sociable," "to be one of the crowd," or "to avoid being left out of the crowd." This implies that drinking is assumed to be an institutionalized means for facilitating sociability. But something special is involved for the teen-agers.

Teen-age drinking is surrounded by an aura of illegality. It is premature from the standpoint of many, if not most, adults, especially if it is not done in a context subject to adult supervision and control. Special precautions on the part of teen-agers to avoid detection are therefore required. Consequently, students themselves place less emphasis on the social facilitation accompanying the use of alcohol than on the group-identification potentialities of its use. While the "wild party" is specified as a common occasion for drinking, the importance of this behavior appears to lie in its symbolizing membership in a group more than anything else. As some teen-agers said:

"Personally, I don't like the flavor of most drinks . . . and the majority of people are against it [teen-age drinking]. I just want to go with the crowd, I guess."

"When the rest of them are drinking and you're the only one that's sitting there and not doing it, it kind of makes you thirsty after a while. At this wedding, I don't know exactly what it was, though us kids had fun doing it and the other kids, I think they were bored stiff because they weren't getting into the fun. Us kids were having lots of fun at this wedding and the other kids didn't; they were bored. . . . Some of us kids had a headache when we woke up the next morning but otherwise the other kids didn't; but we had a lot of fun that night and those other kids didn't."

Wanting to go with the crowd has at least two facets, one positive and the other negative. Some students talked of choosing friends because they liked them, not because they drink or are abstinent; if one's friends drink, then drinking with them may symbolize a common bond of friendship. Other students emphasized a more negative, deterministic interpretation of drinking behavior as a result of peer group identification, as the student who said:

> "I think if you get in certain company, then that will determine what you'll do or not. . . . If you get in certain company that looks down on drinking, then you won't drink."

This oversimple explanation of group determination of behavior does suggest something important: Group identification is important to the teen-ager and the use or avoidance of alcohol is one means of achieving and maintaining such identification.

There were occasional references in the interviews to group pressure to drink, again indicating that drinking is one means by which an individual identifies himself as a member of a group and is so identified by its other members:

> "Pressure is common. There's quite a few that go to these parties and don't drink. They stick to pop. But there are some that do drink. If you don't drink they try to throw one on you or shove one on you. If you say no, right there you're considered chicken. They just forget about you."
>
> "Kids don't drink because they feel they're—oh, I don't know exactly how to say it. They feel that if they don't drink, they're out of the class of kids they are running around with, the popular gang here at school."
>
> "Would I like to drink? I don't drink and I don't think I would like to. I've heard from other people that when they go, they have to drink as everyone else is, standing around with drinks in their hands. I don't want to go because you feel that you have to join in with them and if you don't you aren't exactly sociable."

These student comments are important in the face of evidence that only a small minority of the students in the population studied identified themselves as drinkers and less than one-third of them reported drinking with any degree of consistency. Why there should be sustained pressure from the members of the typical teen-age peer group on nonusers to drink is difficult to explain unless a basic distinction is made between (*1*) what we have called the typical adolescent peer group characterized by at least tentative acceptance that use of alcohol is premature for them and (*2*) the adult-oriented peer group user who considers himself a drinker. In the former one would expect group sanctions against drinking.

For such a group abstinence or, at most, judicious tasting would be an important symbol of conformity to shared expectations about appropriate adolescent behavior. It is only in the latter that the use of drinking behavior as a symbol of group identification would become important. This does not rule out the possibility, however, that drinking may sometimes be used in groups of users to test the willingness of a nonuser to conform to group demands by requiring that both adult and the usual adolescent expectations about drinking be violated.

Unfortunately, it is not possible to achieve closure on this point, primarily because of restrictions placed on the research group. As a condition of gaining access to the public school system, the investigators had to rule out participant observation. Moreover, students were not allowed to identify themselves by name in the interviews; although a number of them indicated a willingness to do so. Consequently, identification of the associates of users and nonusers was not possible.

Nevertheless, the available evidence suggests that teen-age drinking behavior and the teen-ager's identification of himself as a drinker must be seen within the context of social groups which have institutionalized the use of alcohol. It is because drinking is institutionalized behavior in a major segment of our society that the behavior is a symbol which may be presented in various situations as one means of establishing one's self and one's social identity. One important source of motivation for drinking therefore lies in obligatory relationships to others. So long as an individual remains a member of a group which has made institutionalized drinking behavior a mechanism of identification, he may be obligated to present this symbol at the appropriate time regardless of any peculiarly personal sources of motivation to the contrary.[7]

Self-Assessments of Personal Reasons for Drinking

In addition to being asked about the general reasons why students drink, the teen-agers were also asked to assess their personal reasons. "If you drink," they were asked, "what best describes your own

[7] Lemert (49) describes the following situation among Northwest Coast Indians: "When the member of a clan was challenged by a spokesman of another clan to drink down his portion of whiskey or rum, he did so because otherwise he and his clan stood to lose status. In other words, his personal needs had to be subordinated to the claims made upon him by the clan; non-anxious as well as anxious individuals had to conform with the ritual requirements of the situation."

feelings about why you drink?" Table 25 reports the responses of users.

When the responses of boy and girl drinkers are compared, the reasons for drinking they gave were very similar. About half the students, both boys and girls, reported drinking because "I like it." About 40% of the self-designated nondrinkers also made this response. This individualistic explanation of drinking behavior seems to contradict the previous emphasis on the social sources of this behavior, but contradiction is only apparent.

One characteristic of adult role playing in our society is that personal discretion is expected and required, the adult being held personally accountable for his acts by society. The opposite side of this coin is that the individual has a right to be personally accountable for the decision which he himself makes. Moreover, the "pursuit of pleasure" is a positively valued goal. This is reflected, incidentally, in the frequency with which the students selected from their "vocabularies of motives" the particular responses "I wanted to" or "I like to do this" in answer to the question "Why did you do that?" For an individual to assert, "I drink because I like it" reflects in large part an assertion of the right to personal decision about the means to achieve pleasure. This explanation is congruent with the previous observation that the user is predominantly oriented to an identification with adult roles. Additional confirmation of this point is found in two bits of evidence: (*1*) among the users, drinkers were more likely than others to give "I like it" as the reason for their drinking; and (*2*) boys were more likely than girls in each instance to make this assertion.

The second and third most frequently mentioned motives for drinking by users are "to celebrate some special occasion" and "to

TABLE 25.—*Responses By Users to, "If You Drink, Which of the Following Best Describes Your Reason(s)?" By Self-Designation and Sex, in Per Cent**

	Nondrinkers		*Drinkers*	
Reasons	*Boys*	*Girls*	*Boys*	*Girls*
I like it	43	37	55	48
I drink to be with the crowd	25	13	18	22
I drink to celebrate some special occasion	30	44	19	22
I drink when I am unhappy	2	6	8	8
Totals	*100*	*100*	*100*	*100*

* Multiple responses are included in all totals. The number of each type of response is expressed as a percentage of the total number of responses.

be with the crowd," in that order among the nondrinkers and about in the same proportion among the drinkers. Among the former, the girls emphasize the use of alcohol in the celebration of special occasions to a striking degree in contrast to the other users. A small minority of users listed "I drink when I am unhappy" as a reason.

Those who designated themselves as nonusers were asked to indicate their reasons for tasting alcohol, if they had ever done so. About two-thirds of the boys and three-fourths of the girls responded, "to see what it was like." For these students the use of alcohol was considered exploratory. Stated differently, their behavior may be described as anticipatory socialization.[8] The behavior of users and, especially, of the self-designated drinkers who are considered by adults to be adolescents might also be described in these terms. For the user, however, the process is simply further advanced. The exploratory tasting of the nonuser anticipates behavior which is perceived by the teen-ager to be common among persons playing adult roles in the larger society in which he is a member. This does not mean that all tasters will become drinkers as adults. The tasting does suggest that most teen-agers entertain this as a possibility.

Up to this point several aspects of motivation for teen-age drinking have been discussed. Summing up, attention has been directed to a consideration of the status transforming potentialities of alcohol and its use as a means of self-identification and social identification. Some teen-age drinking is clearly related to a transformation of status from adolescence to adulthood. Drinking behavior is also related to peer group identification. For nonusers as well as users tasting or drinking anticipates a pattern of behavior associated with adult role playing. Before other facets of teen-age drinking behavior are considered, it is useful to comment on the effects imputed to the use of alcohol by the students.

Demonstrable and Imputed Effects of Drinking on Behavior

Some, if not most, of the high-school students interviewed were aware that, pharmacologically, alcohol is an anesthetic whose depressant effect on the central nervous system tends to impair

[8] "Anticipatory socialization" is used by Merton and Kitt (61) to describe identification with values assumed to be held by members of a group in which one is not yet a member, in anticipation of becoming a member.

judgment, discrimination, inhibitions and muscular coordination. For example:

"I have read articles that proclaim that it dulls your senses, so that you're slower on your reactions and things like that; that doesn't make you quite as sharp and may make you irritable toward people, say things you don't mean."

"Well, alcohol numbs your senses. They don't have the—I mean, they can't think quick enough to put their foot on the brake or they can't see. They can't see as far, their seeing is a lot less and it numbs their senses a lot . . . I think we studied alcohol in personal and social problems here at school."

Yet in the interviews both users and nonusers were more likely to emphasize personal or social effects of drinking than purely physiological effects. A catalog of "effects" can be abstracted which, if taken at face value, considerably broadens notions about what alcohol is assumed to do to and for people. Such phrases as "feeling high," "floating on air," "freeness," "getting real happy," "getting oomph," and so on, are clearly related to experiences with a physiological base. It is important to note, however, that these experiences are not ends in themselves but are related to the achievement of personally or socially valued goals:

"Quite a number of times kids had been drinking at one of the dances . . . well, a couple of guys came in one night and they were, you know, feeling real happy and there was a cop standing there. They sort of made fun of him, I mean they didn't really do anything and the cop didn't do anything. But they were making fun of him, pointing at him, doing silly things. I can't remember what they were doing but everybody got sort of a big charge out of it. . . ."

"If you have one bottle of beer, sometimes you'll get awfully dizzy on it and two will make you flat drunk. Whereas, if you continue on that, it'll take five or six before you even get to feeling good. . . . I've never gone overboard. I've never got to the stage where I can't walk—but I'm feeling good on Christmas Eve. . . ."

By implication, these teen-agers also attributed to alcohol qualities which "cause" or at least are related to "pleasure," "sociability," "manliness," "conviviality," and so on. Alcohol is perceived to be related to the achievement of personally or socially desirable goals.

W. I. Thomas, (86, *p. 572*) has generalized that, "If men define situations as real, they are real in their consequences." Merton (60, *p. 179*) uses this quotation as a springboard for a discussion of what he calls "self-fulfilling prophecy"; that is, some social behavior is explainable, at least in part, by the fact that the consequences are predicted. Symbols allow some leeway in the perception of environment. Therefore, in understanding the use of alcohol and the effects which it presumably has on the behavior of the drinker, it is important to make a distinction between the demonstrable physiological effects of alcohol and the imputed effects. Lindesmith (50) has noted, for example, that in the treatment of the opiate addict, "the possibility of deception is considered an established fact . . . under certain conditions an addict may be deceived into believing that he is under the influence of the drug though he is actually not, and vice versa" (*p. 32*). He adds: "In other words, nearly all the direct effects of the drug which last beyond a few minutes after the shot are such that they could easily be attributed to other causes if they appeared in isolation. Knowing that he is an addict, the addict ascribes his mental changes to the drug, not because they are recognizable as such but because they accompany the shot" (*p. 35*).

Although it should be stated again that teen-age drinking cannot be equated with the process of drug addiction, how the consequences of drinking conform with expectations is illustrated by the shared prophecy of most teen-agers that alcohol makes one "sociable," "gay," and so on through a whole catalog of imputed effects. As Lindesmith's data would lead one to suspect, some of the effect of alcohol may occasionally be faked. A single illustration from the interviews will make the point sufficiently:

"Kids, especially high-school kids, go berserk, you might say. They get silly about it, you know. And they'll drink it and—like some girls I've known to drink small amounts of it—they'll get real gigglish and silly. They say they're drunk but they're actually not; it's just that they say that they are, so somebody'll think they're smart. . . . It makes them put on false acts and they put on false acts that wouldn't ordinarily do. . . . Kids act that way to get attention in most cases. . . . I've seen a lot of that."

Logically, there is no stopping point in the effects which might be imputed to drinking once the process of symbolic transformation is taken into consideration.[9] This does not mean that the physiological effects of given amounts of alcohol on the nervous

[9] That the possible "effects" of alcohol are much more diverse than is suggested here is documented in the cross-cultural studies summarized in Chapter 2. The "effects" of alcohol on human behavior are, to an important degree, culturally defined.

system may be ignored. It does mean that, when small amounts are involved, the associated behavior cannot be attributed altogether to the pharmacological action of alcohol.

With the implications of this kind of transformation for understanding the effects of drinking on behavior in mind, it is now possible to consider another meaning of drinking in our society which is reflected in the verbalized reasons teen-agers give for their drinking. The data on which these speculative observations are made are admittedly incomplete.

DRINKING AND THE LEGITIMATION OF UNCONVENTIONAL BEHAVIOR

In spite of the fact that alcohol is demonstrably a depressant, some students spoke of the beverage as though it were a stimulant, specifically, an aphrodisiac. This imputed quality of alcohol, for example, underlies the boys' preference for an all–male drinking group. It also underlies the preferences of some of the girls for drinking only at home "where I know I am going to be safe" and the frequently expressed feeling that "it just doesn't look right for girls to drink," especially in mixed groups:

"Well, according to mother, drinking makes people forget their—lose their heads and so forth. . . . We never invite a girl to a party anyway, that kind; and we never mention or do anything around girls. . . . I never get myself in that situation. If a girl tried to drink with us we'd boot her out of the general area, give her the freezeout."

"It doesn't seem right to be drinking in mixed company. 'Cause us guys never drank with a mixed group. I don't think none of the guys would like it either. . . . It just seems not right for girls to drink around boys. They get too wild."

Such similar comments appeared only incidentally in the interviews, since the research group agreed, at the request of the public school administration, not to probe the sex experience of the students. It is relevant to point out, nevertheless, that a similar association between alcohol and sex has been noted by other research.

In their study of almost 17,000 college students, Straus and Bacon (82) found that the students assumed a relationship between drinking and sexual behavior. A majority of both abstainers and drinkers associated drinking with one or another form of sexual behavior, such as petting and necking, sexual excitement, or sexual intercourse. Whether this belief reflected experience or moral indoctrination was not determined.

Straus and Bacon did not speculate about the theoretical implications of these data. Yet at least passing reference to a comment by Margaret Mead on the possible relationship between sex and alcohol in our society seems relevant. Mead speculates (59, *p. 217*) that, in a society which strongly indoctrinates its members against the idea that sex is play and, as such, may be enjoyed, alcohol may facilitate sex play by lowering inhibitions. Although she does not elaborate the point, several additional speculative comments may be made. Inebriety is demonstrably related to the reduction of inhibitions; in part this relationship is explained in terms of pharmacological effects (i.e., the depressant effect on the central nervous system) which have social consequences.[10] But it is equally appropriate to ask, to what extent does the association between sex and alcohol reflect the institutionalization of drinking as a means for facilitating sexual behavior? This question substitutes a sociological question for a physiological one.

The present data are too sketchy to provide an answer to the question. However, the possibility that drinking *is* an institutionalized means for facilitating sexual behavior is certainly suggested in the light of the previous discussion of symbolic transformation and self-fulfilling prophecy. Our impressions and the Straus and Bacon data do suggest that belief in the relationship is widespread. It remains to be determined what significance this belief has for behavior; we have the impression that Margaret Mead's speculation is a lead worth investigating.

Drinking and Aggression

The questionnaire used in the study did not explore the extent to which the teen-agers believed drinking to be related to physical aggression against others or verbalized aggression against society. Comments relevant to this point were only rarely made in the interviews, although other research suggests that drinking and physical aggression are frequently believed to be associated[11] and, in fact, to some extent are related.[12] The most obvious explanation

[10] For example, Clark (11) found, through the use of Thematic Apperception Tests, that sex symbolism increases when persons are under the influence of alcohol.

[11] Straus and Bacon (82, *pp. 186-195*) found this belief among college students, especially in men; the theoretical implications of the absence of this association in women are not explored.

[12] See (95, *p. 49*) for data on "unusual behavior" following drinking. Wattenberg and Moir (91) conclude that "on the basis of [our] findings, we may say that

of the relationship is in terms of the depressant effect of alcohol on the central nervous system and the consequent reduction of inhibitions, judgment and discretion. But, as in the previous comments on alcohol and sexual behavior, an equally interesting question is "To what extent is alcohol an institutionalized means for the expression of aggression in our society?"

The possibility that drinking is institutionalized in our society as a means for legitimating certain types of unconventional behavior appears to warrant exploration in future research. It was noted that during the interviews the teen-agers frequently followed descriptions of unconventional behavior after drinking with humorous comments. It can be observed in our society that the aggressive person who is assumed to be intoxicated is avoided rather than attacked; his behavior is frequently explained away by saying, "he doesn't know what he is doing." To the extent that members of a society treat behavior following drinking as an occasion for humor or avoidance rather than as an occasion for indignation and punishment, drinking may be considered an institutionalized means for breaking the conventions of the society. Alcohol use in such situations legitimates deviant behavior.[13]

Summary

In this chapter a point of view in understanding the motivation to drink has been presented in outline. This orientation emphasized the learning of the significance of a system of symbols with tradi-

heavy drinking by juveniles is closely allied to delinquency in general. It is part of a revolt against grown-ups engaged in by boys who have weak relationships to people and impoverished inner resources." It is important to note that Wattenberg and Moir are not describing the drinking behavior of adolescents in general but adolescents with police records.

[13] In an unpublished paper entitled, "Charisma: The reinterpretation and extension of a concept," one of the authors (G.L.M.) has suggested the possible utility of Max Weber's concept of "charisma" in the analysis of drinking behavior. The rationale for this application is documented in the paper. However, it is pertinent to note here that some uses of alcohol do appear (*1*) to legitimate non-ordinary and "revolutionary" behavior vis-à-vis the established social order and (*2*) to be associated with the belief that alcohol has a power over the human being over which he has only limited control, i.e., alcohol is "superhuman." These are two key characteristics of Weber's concept applied in a new context. If the routinization of charisma is taken into account, then the "revolutionary" aspect of charismatic claims may be viewed as a mechanism which is functional to some degree in maintaining an established social order. Inebriety, in this instance, becomes a safety valve by permitting occasions for the expression of aggression toward persons and values which would ordinarily not be permitted.

tional meanings. In social interaction a person learns to define situations and, having defined them, to mobilize his energy and direct it selectively toward his environment. He does this because he has learned what significance certain presented symbols should have for him. Why certain symbols come to be invested with peculiar significance is explained at least in part by three factors: (*1*) the value in desirability of various statuses in social groups; (*2*) the individual's self-image which emerges in interaction with others; and (*3*) his status aspirations within the society.

A "vocabulary of motives" provides a basis for insight into the traditional meaning of particular symbols.

When teen-agers specified the "reasons" why adults drink, they agreed that drinking behavior is explained by its relationship to sociability, pleasure and anxiety reduction. In this way, the students related drinking to positive social values.

When teen-agers explained the drinking of their peers, they emphasized "acting smart," "being one of the crowd," and "avoiding being left out." The user added that he drank personally "because I like it," while the nonuser added, "I wanted to see what it was like."

When placed within the context of an age-graded social system, these more obvious meanings of drinking to the teen-ager also suggest certain meanings which are less obvious, four of which have been discussed: (*1*) status transformation; (*2*) group identification; (*3*) anticipatory socialization; and (*4*) legitimating of unconventional behavior.

Chapter 6

SOME CONCLUDING OBSERVATIONS

ALCOHOL USE is a socially structured and culturally defined pattern of behavior to which almost all adolescents in our society are exposed in the process of growing up and with which most of them sooner or later experiment. This perspective proved useful in understanding much of what the teen-agers in this study reported they thought about and did with alcoholic beverages. Whether or not these high-school students were currently using beverage alcohol, none of them had to invent the idea of drinking. Some drinking was perceived by most of them as a usual aspect of adult role playing. In contrast, alcohol use was not perceived by them as a usual aspect of behavior by adolescents. These students shared common definitions about both where and why most adults drink, and these definitions clearly indicated the legitimacy of some drinking behavior. For in spite of the recognition that some adults use alcoholic beverages as drugs to tranquilize anxiety and tension, the predominant image of alcohol among these teen-agers suggested a social beverage associated with conviviality and the celebration of social events rather than a drug associated with anxiety reduction. Alcohol was perceived as capable of doing something *for* the drinker and not just *to* him.

If adult roles are perceived as having alcohol use as a normal component, in contrast to the abstinence perceived as normative for the teen-ager, then one might expect that the teen-ager's identification of himself primarily as an adult or primarily as an adolescent would be an important variable in determining patterns of drinking or abstinence. In fact, this is what was found. Those teen-agers still in high school who were users were more likely to indicate an identification with or involvement in adult roles than were the nonusers. Among users these characteristics were more pronounced among self-identified drinkers than among nondrinkers. The playing of or identification with adult roles is in part a function of age: the older the teen-ager, the greater the probability that he will orient himself away from extensive involvement in school-related activity. Social status is also a relevant factor. The life experiences of the lower-status young person, for example, tend to encourage an early claim to adult status and the playing of adult roles sooner than the young person socialized in a middle-status family. Age and social status, therefore, theoretically should be and are related to observed differences in the probability that adolescents of various ages and variously placed in the social structure will be users and, if users, drinkers. In addition to age and social status, sex is a third factor which illustrates drinking as socially structured and culturally dependent. In this study, rather consistent differences were found between what boys and girls reported they thought about and did with alcohol. With regard to alcohol use, a familiar double standard of expectations was applied to boys and girls. Boys not only were more likely than girls to be users; they were also expected to be.

A perspective which views some alcohol use by adolescents as an integral part of the process of growing up in a society in which a majority of adults integrate alcohol use with the fabric of their own social life does more than explain why about one-third of the boys and one-fifth of the girls in this study were found to be users. The perspective of this study would also lead one to hypothesize that through time the majority status of the nonuser and the minority status of the user will be reversed. Our confidence that a study of the patterns of alcohol use and abstinence among the subjects in this study, say ten years later, will support this hypothesis is based on the observation that while most children in our society are assumed to be abstinent, a majority of adults in our society report that they use alcohol. For particular segments of the population—a predominantly Mormon community would be a case in point—this expectation would not hold. However, the fact that a majority of the young people in this study perceived that most adults legitimately integrate the use of alcohol with their behavior in some way would lead one to conclude that the young people in this study will not prove to be an exception. The expectation is that sooner or later the nonusers will constitute a minority. Furthermore, this study would suggest the hypothesis that the out-of-school teenagers (the drop-outs) would be found to have a significantly higher proportion of users than those in school. Alcohol use would tend to be one of the concomitants of their dissociation from the more closely supervised social world of the adolescent, which is peculiarly represented by the high-school social system, and their positive identification with the prerogatives and responsibilities usually associated with adulthood.

This study, then, while apparently describing how a minority of students have come to use alcohol, actually provides some explanation of why a majority of them eventually will drink. In focusing attention on why a minority already do use alcohol and a majority eventually will, this research has tended to ignore two interesting and important categories of students in high school: (*1*) those who not only are observed to be abstinent currently, but who probably will remain so into and through adulthood; and (*2*) those who already are or are likely to experience personal and social complications as a result of their drinking.

Although most studies on alcohol use provide some incidental information about the abstainer, he has rarely been the subject of systematic study. Knowing that the probability of use, for example, is higher in cities, among men, and among persons identified with Catholicism and Judaism, necessarily tells us that the probability of finding abstainers concentrated in rural areas, among women and Protestants is high. Genevieve Knupfer (45) summarizes the limited research that has been done on the adult abstainer and reports that he is likely to have a rural background, abstaining parents and strong religious convictions which include belief that all drinking is harmful. Specifically she concludes that abstainers "have fathers in blue-collar occupations; both parents disapprove of drinking; neither parent drank; they are over 40; they are less sociable than drinkers; they are more religious in terms both of church attendance and statements about the importance of religion; they themselves disapprove heartily of drinking" (45, *p. 6*). Knupfer could not, from her data, demonstrate substantial psychological differences between abstainers and drinkers. From such a description the inference is invited that limited social mobility, a narrowly defined social environment, consistent exposure to significant adults who are abstainers, and support for abstinence from important sanctioning agencies in the environment, such as the church, are factors which would give continuing support to the patterns of abstinence which are characteristic of the great majority of early adolescents in our society. In a highly mobile society in which a majority of adults use alcohol at least sometimes and in which the major sanctioning agencies, including religious organizations, do not consistently support total abstinence, only a minority of adolescents would be exposed to those conditions supporting abstinence into and through adulthood. The fact remains that a sizable part of the adult population (an estimated one-third) is abstinent, and this should not be ignored. Nevertheless, we know very little about either how or why the pattern of abstinence is sustained as a minority position in adulthood. This study does not contribute very much to our understanding of this point, although the need for such research among teen-agers is clearly indicated.

At the other extreme we have had very little to say about the teen-ager whose use of alcohol calls attention to him precisely because his behavior falls outside the patterns of use observed among his age peers who also drink. The minority of teen-agers who experience social or personal complications as a result of their drinking have been no more adequately studied than the minority of teen-agers who will as adults remain abstinent. Various studies have commented on the prevalence of social complications associated with drinking by teen-agers and young adults. Straus and Bacon (82, *pp. 156 ff.*), for example, devote some attention to what they call "the potential problem drinker" among collegians (older adolescents). These authors developed a scale of social complications which included four items: (*1*) failure to meet social obligations; (*2*) damage to friendships; (*3*) accident or injury; and (*4*) formal punishment or discipline. Sixty-six per cent of the men who were users and 85% of the women among those who reported drinking had experienced no complications as a result of alcohol use. Of the 34% of the men who reported some complications, only 6% had experienced accident or injury, or formal punishment or discipline. Less than 1% of the women had experienced complications of this seriousness, out of the 15% who reported at least one complication.

Surveys of drinking behavior and attitudes among high-school students (see Chapter 2) have generally reported that between 1 and 5% of the students with an established pattern of alcohol use indicate that they drink extensively and have experienced social or personal complications as a result of their drinking behavior. In high school, as in college, most students, therefore, do not appear to organize their lives in a significant way around drinking, and special problems associated with drinking tend to be the exception rather than the rule. These studies give some indication of the prevalence of complications associated with the drinking of some teen-agers, but they do not really give us any understanding of why a persistent minority of young people exhibit peculiarities in their drinking behavior that lead to complications.

It is possible that the adolescent of high-school age who is most likely to experience complications as a result of his drinking is more likely than others to have dropped out of school. Hollingshead's 1949 study of Elmtown (36, *pp. 408 ff.*) is the only available systematic study of the drinking behavior of this type of student. Although Hollingshead refers to the drinking behavior of the drop-out as "delinquent" and notes that the use of alcoholic beverages is much more common among drop-outs than among those who remain in school, he does not indicate that the drinking behavior of the drop-out is peculiarly associated with complications.

In the absence of research that has focused specifically on "problem drinking" among adolescents, studies of delinquency might be expected to provide information about a segment of the population which is an especially high risk group for experiencing complications as a result of their drinking. The teen-ager who has been judged by the criminal justice procedure to be delinquent has not been found necessarily to experience complications as a result of drinking. The fact that in some instances the young person who uses beverage alcohol at all is considered by definition as delinquent only confuses the issue. Although studies of delinquent gangs and subcultures have not ordinarily considered the use of alcohol systematically, when the matter has been considered, alcohol use has not been found to play a particularly prominent part in the subculture of delinquents. For example, in a recent monograph summarizing delinquency research in the United States, Cloward and Ohlin (12, *Ch. 15*) note that while drunkenness among adolescents is frequently dealt with as a delinquent act by criminal justice authorities, drinking is not typically a central activity or focus of gang behavior. Regular and heavy use of alcohol is not a condition of group acceptance among delinquent gangs typically; but, more than this, inebriety or the euphoric states induced by the use of alcohol or narcotics are considered inimical to the welfare of such groups and therefore discouraged.

All deviant or delinquent children, whether their problem is alcohol or something else, do share a common problem. Cloward and Ohlin assert that these children have found available personal and legitimate social resources inadequate for the development and maintenance of a conception of self which is satisfactory to themselves and others. Attempts to deal with this inadequacy may take the form of tightly organized criminal behavior, transitory conflict behavior, or still more transitory and loosely organized escapist behavior characterized by "the cat looking for kicks" in such experiences as narcotics, sex and alcohol use. These authors emphasize that most delinquent boys cannot be adequately characterized simply as emotionally confused, normless or erratic. A minority can be so characterized, and those who can are more likely than others to be found in the type of delinquent subcultures which the authors label "escapist." It is here that alcohol use is most likely to play a prominent part and to be associated with personal and social complications for the drinker.

The youngster who participates in the escapist type of delinquent subculture appears to be the product of a double failure. He is a social failure in that he has not found peers with whom he can achieve a successful solution of the discrepancy between his goals and the means at his disposal for achieving them. He is a personal failure insofar as he is unable to attribute the source of difficulty to others or to his environment and therefore unable to handle the sense of guilt associated with failure. This isolation in turn reinforces the probability that he will continue to fail.

Studies of delinquency, then, by implication reinforce one of the basic implications of this study. Deviant drinking behavior is neither characteristic nor an integral part of the typical teen-ager's drinking behavior, in fact not even of that segment of the adolescent population most likely to be antagonistic toward adult values and adult control, the delinquent. The drinking behavior of some delinquents may be associated with complications which are detrimental to their physical, emotional and social functioning; but this experience is atypical. The "cat looking for kicks," whose behavior is likely to involve the use of narcotics or alcohol, is a minority within a minority. Moreover, studies of delinquency emphasize that social and cultural factors—the existence of organized groups to provide models for behavior, shared values and norms, interaction within the family, discrepancy between important social goals and the sources available to achieve them—form the context both for maximizing or minimizing problems of personal adjustment and for providing various more or less satisfactory opportunities for their resolution. For a minority of young people, patterns of drinking which do result in complications are learned. The experience of a minority, however, should not be confused with the drinking behavior of the majority of teen-age drinkers. All available studies indicate that complications are not typically associated with their drinking.

The use of alcohol is not ordinarily the pivot around which the life of the adolescent in high school revolves. This is not to say that there are no problems associated with alcohol use for the student of high-school age or that the problems that do exist are inconsequential. The only point to be made is that problem behavior associated with alcohol use among teen-agers is the exception rather than the rule.

In sum, this study has emphasized the experience of the majority of teen-agers in high school who, in the process of socialization, have come or will shortly come to identify themselves with adult role playing and who have or will soon appropriate to themselves the prerogatives of adult status. Among these prerogatives is the right to use beverage alcohol. It has been shown how such factors as age, sex and social status are related to the process of transforming the dependent behavior of the child into the increasingly independent behavior of the adult. Understanding the process by which a majority of teen-agers come to use beverage alcohol should help provide the needed perspective for future research on the two neglected minority groups in research on alcohol use—the teen-ager who will remain totally and permanently abstinent, and the one who will experience complications as a result of his drinking.

The restriction of attention to the behavior of the emergent majority of these teen-agers is a limitation which should be kept in mind in interpreting the results. But there are obviously other limitations which should be reemphasized at this point. What has been said about the young people whose behavior and attitudes have been reported in these pages cannot simply be generalized to all teen-agers without due caution. Some teen-agers in the community in which the research was done are obviously not represented—the drop-outs. Moreover, while the middle-sized Midwestern community being studied had no characteristics which clearly set it apart from other communities, there is no demonstrated basis for assuming that its adolescents are representative of adolescents in high school everywhere.

The real strength of the study, however, does not lie in the ability to generalize from the data about the prevalence of drinking behavior and attitudes among these teen-age high-school students. The concern of this study has not been primarily with the prevalence of drinking, but with understanding the process whereby the use of alcohol becomes or does not become an integral part of the behavior of young people. Therefore, it has not been argued on the basis of this study that the proportion of young people found to be using alcohol while still in high school can be generalized to some other community. Rather it has been argued that drinking behavior among teen-agers, wherever it is found, will typically be associated with the increasing identification of the young person with adult status if adulthood is perceived as involving some use of beverage alcohol. It is important to note that the hypothesis does not state that a teen-ager will come to drink simply as a result of growing up. His drinking behavior is associated with growing up in an environment in which an important status to which he legitimately aspires, that of becoming an adult, is perceived typically as involving alcohol use.

An adolescent does not have to invent the idea of drinking; he learns it. Some alcohol use is probably involved in growing up in a society in which most adults drink.

Appendix I

Notes on Methods and Procedures

The data reported herein were collected by the use of a pretested questionnaire and supplemented by the use of tape-recorded individual interviews. Both of these procedures have specific advantages and disadvantages, but we believe that the combination of the two methods in large part compensated for the specific limitations of each.

Once a problem is operationally defined, the successive choices made by the research team progressively limit the information which can be obtained. For various reasons decisions were made, sometimes by us and sometimes by others, which affected our analysis. Consideration of these choices may help the reader to interpret the results with reference to his special point of view.

Perhaps social research upon certain types of behavior, such as alcohol use in a teen-age high-school population, raises more ethical problems to be decided in the conduct of the research than is true of less value-loaded problems. Such problems were encountered in our research and, in response, several decisions were made which we feel limit the completeness of our conclusions.

In retrospect, certain of the decisions of the local school administration which seemed overcautious at the time now seem to us to be a reasonable discharge of their primary duty to the young people in the schools. For example, no student was allowed to participate without the written approval of his or her parent or guardian. Each student was assigned a number by the school administration, and the research team used only these numbers in the identification of data. Information about friendship patterns and group processes as they relate to drinking was, therefore, unavailable.

Our data do not provide extensive information about two other social phenomena which may enter into variations in motivation patterns underlying alcohol use: religious and sexual behavior. Unfortunately, short-sighted and sometimes bigoted individuals do sometimes misuse data reporting differences in behavior among groups with one or another religious identification. This fact is reason enough for the caution displayed by school officials. We nevertheless regretted this loss of information which would have made our analysis more complete.

The decision not to explore the relationship between alcohol use and sexual behavior was made reluctantly. One of our pretest groups consisted of teen-age males in the State Industrial School (a custodial school for delinquents committed by court order), among whom sexual delinquency and alcohol use appeared to be related, although both appeared to be common products of personal and social demoralization. We did not pursue this relationship for several reasons. Additional pretest data from a high-school population indicated that a less marked relationship existed between sexual and drinking behavior among students than among the delinquents. Although at first we felt the question of sufficient importance to pursue, the possible effects of doing so upon the primary goals of the research led us to drop this idea.

The use of participant observation study of drinking behavior of either, or both, students and drop-outs was discussed, but we felt that the social implications of this method would be undesirable. If we used a teen-age participant observer, we would be asking him to engage in illegal behavior; if we used an adult, who presumably would be mature enough to make a responsible decision, we would in effect be encouraging teen-age drinking by making it appear that it had adult approval.

Our major methodological decision was to secure data by questionnaires and to follow up with an intensive interview of a selected sample of students who had completed the questionnaire. In the analysis, these two distinctive types of information have been juxtaposed in order to provide a better understanding of the motivational patterns underlying drinking behavior.

We chose the questionnaire method in order to secure data from all the students in the public high schools of the community and then to draw samples from this population for closer study. We felt that a statistical description of the groups studied, their aspirations and social participation, their conception of their school and community, and their perception of community drinking patterns would indicate the more obscure forces affecting their attitudes and behaviors concerning alcohol. This questionnaire was developed from the self-reports of college students and male delinquents and pretested on a small high-school student body. In both instances students were interviewed in groups to find out specific interpretations of the questionnaire items and to secure suggestions for making the questions more meaningful.

After the administration of the questionnaire to the study group, and the preliminary tabulation of results, a sample of students was selected for interviewing. This was done to check on the interpretation of the questions, the meaning of the answers and upon individual motivational patterns in those areas that seemed significant from the preliminary tabulations.

Appendix II

The Questionnaire

FORM 1

Student no. ....

1. Please write the name of your school here ....

2. Please write the number of your homeroom here ....

3. Indicate your sex by drawing a circle around the appropriate number.
   Male 1
   Female 2

4. Indicate your grade in school. 11th 1 12th 2

5. What was your age at last birthday:

14, and under	1	18	5
15	2	19	6
16	3	20, or over	7
17	4		

6. Write the correct number of older or younger brothers and sisters you have in the appropriate space. (Be sure to write the number on each line. If you have none, write none.)
   Younger brothers and sisters .... Older brothers and sisters ....

7. Are your parents living? Both........ Father only........ Mother only........ Neither........
   If both are living, are they: Living together........ Separated........ Divorced........

8. With whom do you live most of the time?

Both parents	1	Mother and stepfather	5
Father only	2	Foster parents	6
Mother only	3	Other relatives	7
Father and stepmother	4	Others, not relatives	8

9. Who contributes most to the support of your family? (If you do not live with either or both of your parents, answer for the family with which you are now living.)
   Father 1
   Mother 2
   Father and mother equally 3
   Some other person (who?) ....

10. What does the person mentioned in question 9 above do for a living? (Write in the name of his or her occupation.) ....
    If he is employed, for whom does he work? ....

11. Describe as accurately as possible what this person makes or does on the job. (What does he do at work.) ....

12. Please look at the map of [X City] below, make a check mark in the Census

Tract in which you live. If you live outside the city, please write in the name of the school district in which you live ....

[Reproduction of map omitted]

Some people are paid for work in making things by the number of pieces they turn out. This is called "payment by piece rate." Others are paid according to the time they put in on the job, that is, so much per hour or per day. This is called "payment by wage rate." Others are paid a flat sum each week, every two weeks, or once a month and the hours they work are not checked. This is called "payment by salary rate." Others receive income from farming or business operations in the form of profits from things they own and sell. This is called "earning by profits." Others are paid for selling things that others own; this is called "earning by commission." Still others set a charge for the personal services they give. This is called "earning by fee." Finally, many people get returns from the money that they put into shares or bonds of businesses other than their own. This is called "earning by dividends on investments." In answering the following question, circle the number of the answer below that best describes how the person mentioned in 9 above receives most of his income.

13. In what way is the greater proportion of your father's income (or the income of the other person mentioned in question 9) reckoned? Please circle the best answer.

    (2) Earning by dividend on investment
    (3) Earning by fee or commission
    (1) Other (describe) ....
    (4) Payment by salary rate
    (5) Payment by piece rate

14. Does this person do any other kind of work (in addition to that described in question 10) to earn money? Circle the correct answer. Yes....1 No....2
    If yes, what other kind of work? ....

15. In addition to this person, does *anyone else* contribute to the support of your family? Yes....1 No....2

16. If yes, describe as accurately as possible what each one does on the job.

    (a) Mother ....
    (b) Brothers ....
    (c) Sisters ....
    (d) Myself ....
    (e) Other persons ....
    (f) Unemployment compensation ......
    (g) Welfare agencies ....

17. Do you get spending money or an allowance from your parents? Please circle the correct answers. (0) No, or hardly ever, (1) Yes, regularly, (2) Yes, when I ask for it.

18. Do you earn any money by working at home, or away from home? (0) No, or hardly ever, (1) Yes, working at home, (2) Yes, working away from home.

19. Would you please indicate the approximate amount of spending money you have during the week? (0) None, (1) One dollar or less, (2) Two dollars, but less than five, (3) Five dollars, but less than ten, (4) Ten dollars, but less than fifteen, (5) Fifteen dollars, but less than twenty, (6) Twenty dollars, or more.

20. Do you think your father's occupation would be a good life's work for you? (If you are a girl, do you think it would be a good life's work for your future husband?) (0) No good at all, (1) Not very good, (2) Fair, (3) Good, (4) Very good.

21. If you had your choice, what kind of life work would you most like to do?
....

22. What kind of life work do you actually expect, not hope, to do?
....

23. How far in school did your father go? (Answer for the head of the family with whom you live.)

Went to college and to graduate school	1	Did not go beyond seventh grade	6
Went to college	2	Did not go beyond third grade	7
Graduated from high school	3	Went to technical or business school	8
Did not finish high school	4	Other	9
Finished the eighth grade	5		

If other, specify ....

24. How much more education do you expect to get? Please circle the correct answer. (0) Will not finish high school, (1) Will finish high school only, (2) Will go to college, (3) Will go to graduate school after graduating from college, (4) Will go to technical or business school, (5) Don't know.

25. If you will not go to college when you finish high school, which of the following best describes your plans on leaving high school? (0) Get a full time job, (1) Get a full time job and go to night school, (2) Go to a business or secretarial school, (3) Go to a barber or beauty school, (4) Go to a technical or vocational school, (5) Join the army, navy, or air force, or one of the women's branches of the armed services, (6) Don't know.

26. How many times do you attend regular religious services in an average month?
....

27. How would you place your family's interest in religious activities on the following scale? Please circle the best answer.

No interest	0	High interest	3
Very little interest	1	Very high interest	4
Some interest	2		

28. If you attend church services, which of the following descriptive activities best describe the church which you usually attend?

(a) Please circle one of the following:
(1) Usually has over 400 in attendance at Sunday morning services
(2) Usually has between 100 and 400 in attendance at Sunday morning services
(3) Usually has less than 100 in attendance at Sunday morning services

(b) Please circle one of the following:
(1) Church provides regular worship services only
(2) Church provides for youth activities
(3) Church also provides organized educational and recreational facilities

(c) Please circle one of the following:
(1) Minister frequently asks a single member of the congregation to say a prayer during regular worship services
(2) Minister rarely, if ever, asks a single member of the congregation to say a prayer during regular worship services

(d) Please circle one of the following:
(1) Minister was trained in theological school
(2) Minister is a high-school graduate
(3) Minister works at some other occupation besides serving a church

29a. Would you please circle any of the following high-school organizations to which you belong?

(1) Hi-Y
(2) Y-Teens
(3) Scripture Club
(4) Bible Club
(5) Newman Club
(6) Badminton Club
(7) Football Club
(8) Mermaid Club
(9) Girls Varsity Club
(10) Varsity Lettermen
(11) Tumbling
(12) Girls Athletic Association
(13) Spanish Club
(14) Latin Club
(15) French Club
(16) Bridge Club
(17) Chess Club
(18) Music Appreciation Club
(19) Drama Club
(20) Paint Splashers Club
(21) Glee Club
(22) Model Club
(23) Rifle Club
(24) Projector Club
(25) Camera Club
(26) Science Club
(27) Chemistry Club
(28) Girl's Social
(29) Etiquette Club
(30) Key Club
(31) Commercial Club
(32) Future Homemakers
(33) Future Teachers
(34) Future Nurses

29b. Would you please circle any of the following high-school activities in which you participate?

(35) Student Council
(36) School newspaper
(37) School annual
(38) Girls' League
(39) Class play
(40) Honor Society
(41) Band
(42) Choir

29c. Would you please circle any of the following school teams of which you are a member?

(43) Football
(44) Basketball
(45) Baseball
(46) Wrestling
(47) Golf
(48) Tennis
(49) Swimming
(50) Track
(51) Cross Country

30. Check the list of organizations, activities, and teams in question 29. If for any reason you would like to participate in one, or more, of these, please write the number or numbers in this space ....

31. Would you please circle any of the following types of nonschool activities in which you are active?

(1) Group sports
(2) Young people's religious groups
(3) Musical or artistic group activities
(4) Community activities
(5) Boy Scouts or Girl Scouts

32a. We often group individuals into types, because they have similar habits and occupations. Would you please circle any of the following types, if any, you would like to be like?

(1) Some types of high-school students
(2) Teachers in my school
(3) Some specific individuals of my age
(4) Well known adults in my community
(5) Some well known public officials
(6) Some personalities of television or movies
(7) Some type of athlete

32b. The things I consider important in a person I would like to be like are: (Please circle the appropriate choices)

(1) How much he stands up for his beliefs
(2) How well he can convince others of his beliefs
(3) How well his life expresses his beliefs
(4) How successful he has been in his chosen life's work
(5) How much he has achieved in material success
(6) How much he contributes to his community, or country
(7) How much he is liked and admired by others
(8) How well he can get along with others
(9) How considerate he is of others' feelings

33. Sometimes people talk about upper, middle, and lower classes in the community, and say that a family is one of these. To which one of the following do you think your family belongs, if any?

Lower class .... 1 Upper class 4
Lower middle class .... 2 Some other 5
Upper middle class .... 3 Don't know 6
If some other, how would you describe it? ....

34. Do you usually run around with a group of good friends or a "gang" of boys or girls your own age? Yes........1 No........2
If you do, what are the names of some of these people? (Name as many as you wish.)

....

35. List the name of five students that you would select to represent your high school at a conference to discuss students' problems. (Assume that your school would be judged by these students.)

....

36. High-school students with similar backgrounds and interests usually form groups, and the members of these groups develop ideas about their group and other groups. Would you please circle the most appropriate characteristic below which most nearly represents the standard by which you judge your group, and other groups in your school?
I usually classify student groups:

(1) By the amount of social activities in which they participate
(2) By the organizations to which they belong
(3) By the type of behavior that characterizes the members of the group
(4) By how high their standards of good conduct are
(5) By the social standing of the parents of the group

37. Compared with others of your age, how well do you usually feel you are dressed?
    (1) Extremely well
    (2) Better than average student
    (3) About average
    (4) Below average

38. Whose opinion counts most when you are deciding what to wear?
    (1) Older brother
    (2) Older sister
    (3) Younger brother
    (4) Younger sister
    (5) Father
    (6) Mother
    (7) Fellows younger than I
    (8) Girls younger than I
    (9) Fellows about my age
    (10) Girls about my age
    (11) Fellows a little older than I
    (12) Girls a little older than I
    No one
    Other person (Specify—"my aunt," "my cousin," etc.) ....

39. Do you ever want to know whether other people like or dislike your clothes?
    (1) Never
    (2) Once in a while
    (3) Often
    (4) Very often

40. It bothers me when people talk behind my back. (Check the response below which most nearly indicates how you feel about this statement.)
    (1) Strongly agree
    (2) Agree
    (3) Uncertain
    (4) Disagree
    (5) Strongly disagree

FORM 2

Student No. ....

The questions in this form are asked in order to find out your opinions about the use of alcoholic beverages. There are no right answers, your opinion is as correct as any other student's.

In the question below would you please give your estimate of the proportion of people in your community who can be classified as regular drinkers, infrequent drinkers, and people who do not drink. In your thinking, please distinguish between adults, high-school students, and "drop-outs" (those people of your age who have dropped out of school).

Please circle the correct proportion

1. In your opinion, what proportion of adults drink regularly? (0) None, (1) One-fourth, (2) One-half, (3) Three-fourths, (4) All, or nearly all.

2. In your opinion, what proportion of adults drink sometimes, but not regularly? (0) None, (1) One-fourth, (2) One-half, (3) Three-fourths, (4) All, or nearly all.

3. In your opinion, what proportion of adults never drink, or rarely drink? (0) None, (1) One-fourth, (2) One-half, (3) Three-fourths, (4) All, or nearly all.

4. In your opinion, what proportion of high-school students drink regularly? (0) None, (1) One-fourth, (2) One-half, (3) Three-fourths, (4) All, or nearly all.

5. In your opinion, what proportion of high-school students drink sometimes, but not regularly? (0) None, (1) One-fourth, (2) One-half, (3) Three-fourths, (4) All, or nearly all.

6. In your opinion, what proportion of high-school students never drink, or rarely drink? (0) None, (1) One-fourth, (2) One-half, (3) Three-fourths, (4) All, or nearly all.

7. In your opinion, what proportion of "drop-outs" drink regularly? (0) None, (1) One-fourth, (2) One-half, (3) Three-fourths, (4) All, or nearly all.

8. In your opinion, what proportion of "drop-outs" drink sometimes, but not regularly? (0) None, (1) One-fourth, (2) One-half, (3) Three-fourths, (4) All, or nearly all.

9. In your opinion, what proportion of "drop-outs" never drink, or rarely drink? (0) None, (1) One-fourth, (2) One-half, (3) Three-fourths, (4) All, or nearly all.

The following suggested reasons are some of those given by people to explain why they drink. Please read them over, and use them to answer the next nine questions. Select the three *you* consider the most common reasons why adults, high-school students, and "drop-outs" use alcohol.

From the list below, select the numbers which represent the reasons which you think are the best answers to the following questions

(1) To be sociable with others
(2) Afraid of being left out of the group
(3) Not enough supervision, or discipline
(4) For pleasure, or recreation
(5) To celebrate some occasion
(6) Their parents don't care
(7) Because their family drinks
(8) They want to be one of the crowd
(9) They think it is all right
(10) It is a habit with them
(11) To prove they can hold it
(12) They think it is smart to drink
(13) They are afraid they will be considered sissies if they don't drink
(14) To get rid of their worries
(15) Domestic, or family troubles
(16) To see what it is like
(17) Financial problems
(18) They are rejected by others
(19) To get attention from others
(20) They are bored and have nothing better to do
(21) They are unhappy or sick
(22) Because they don't know any better
(23) To act grownup
(24) It makes them feel important
(25) They are afraid they will be considered squares if they don't drink

10. The most important reason that causes adults to drink is ....

11. The second most important reason that causes adults to drink is ....

12. The third most important reason that causes adults to drink is ....

13. The most important reason that causes high-school students to drink is ....

14. The second most important reason that causes high-school students to drink is ....

15. The third most important reason that causes high-school students to drink is ....

16. The most important reason that causes "drop-outs" to drink is ....

17. The second most important reason that causes "drop-outs" to drink is ....

18. The third most important reason that causes "drop-outs" to drink is ....

The following suggested occasions for drinking are some of those given by people to explain the situation in which they drink. Please read them over and use them to answer the next three questions. Select the three you consider the most likely occasion on which adults, high-school students, and "drop-outs" will drink.

From the list below, select the three most appropriate answers to the following questions

(1) At dances
(2) At parties
(3) When relatives visit
(4) After school events
(5) At weddings
(6) Only on special occasions
(7) New Year's, Christmas, or other holidays
(8) At a friend's home
(9) When they entertain at home
(10) Daily drinking in the home, taverns, bars, or night clubs
(11) At games, or other sporting events
(12) Card parties
(13) On fishing or hunting trips
(14) On weekends, for recreation
(15) With parents or relatives
(16) At wild parties
(17) At beer parties
(18) On all-night parties
(19) On teen-age parties
(20) When they associate with older people
(21) On unsupervised parties or gatherings

19. The three occasions at which adults are most likely to drink are ...., ..., and ....

20. The three occasions at which high-school students are most likely to drink are ...., ..., and ....

21. The three occasions at which "drop-outs" are most likely to drink are ...., ..., and ....

From the list below, select the three most appropriate answers to the next three questions

(1) At dances or parties
(2) At bars, nightclubs, road-houses, and taverns
(3) In parks, at lakes, or outdoor recreational places
(4) At home
(5) When entertaining at home
(6) In a friend's home
(7) In private clubs
(8) At unsupervised parties
(9) In secret, where others can't know
(10) In an automobile
(11) In the country, on back roads
(12) At summer cottages

22. The places in which adults are most likely to drink are ...., ..., and ....

23. The places in which high-school students are most likely to drink are ...., ..., and ....

24. The places in which "drop-outs" are most likely to drink are ...., ..., and ....

25. Do you consider yourself as a person who drinks? Yes.............. No............... .

26. If the answer to question 25 is no, have you ever tasted alcoholic beverages? Yes............... No............... .

27. If you consider yourself a drinker, how frequently do you drink?

Heavily	1	Sometimes	3
Often	2	Rarely	4

28. If you drink beer, would you please indicate the amount you drink in an average week, including the weekend, by circling the correct answer? (0) Never, (1) Rarely drink beer – less than one bottle per week, (2) Less than three bottles in an average week, (3) From three to six bottles of beer in an average week, (4) More than six bottles in an average week.

29. If you drink whisky, would you please indicate the amount you drink in an average week, including the weekend, by circling the correct answer? (0) Never, or rarely drink whisky, (1) Less than three shot glasses, or highballs, (2) Between three and six shot glasses, or highballs, (3) More than six shot glasses, or highballs.

30. If you drink wine, would you please indicate the amount you drink in an average week, including the weekend, by circling the correct answer? (0) Never, or rarely drink wine, (1) Less than three wine glasses, (2) From three to six wine glasses, (3) More than six wine glasses.

31. If you drink mixed drinks, in addition to whisky highballs, would you please indicate the amount you drink in an average week, including the weekend, by circling the correct answer? (0) Never, or rarely drink mixed drinks, (1) Less than three mixed drinks, (2) From three to six mixed drinks, (3) More than six mixed drinks.

32. If you drink, which of the following describe the situation(s) in which you drink? Circle the appropriate answers. (1) When I am with a group of friends, (2) When I am with my parents, (3) When I am with relatives, (4) When I am at a party where drinking is going on, (5) At some special event, (6) On holidays, such as New Year or Christmas, (7) On weekends, for recreation, (8) On fishing or hunting trips, or vacations, (9) Anywhere I can.

33. If you drink, which of the following reasons best describe your feelings about drinking? Please circle the correct response. (1) I drink because I like it, (2) I drink to be with the crowd, (3) I drink when I am unhappy, (4) I drink because I have older friends who drink, (5) I drink to celebrate some special occasion.

34. If you don't drink, but have tasted alcohol, which of the following describe the situations on which you tasted alcohol? Please circle the appropriate answers. (1) I tasted it when I was with a group of friends, (2) With my parents, (3) With some relatives, (4) At some special occasion, (5) At a party where

drinking was going on, (6) On a holiday, (7) On a fishing or hunting trip, or vacation.

35. If you don't drink, but have tasted alcohol, which of the following best describe your reason for tasting it? Please circle the correct responses. (1) To see what it was like, (2) On a dare, (3) Because a friend urged me to taste it, (4) To see if I could do it, (5) I was interested because it is forbidden, (6) I was tricked into thinking it was something else, (7) I was angry at my parents or close friends.

36. Whether you drink or not, which of the following best describe *your* personal opinion of drinking by people of your own age? Please circle the best answer.

    (1) Drinking is all right
    (2) Drinking is all right, if one doesn't get the habit
    (3) Drinking is all right, if one doesn't drink too much and lose self-control
    (4) Drinking is all right, unless one is driving
    (5) Drinking is all right, if one drinks only on weekends
    (6) Drinking is all right, if one only drinks on holidays, or special occasions
    (7) Drinking is all right, if one only drinks to be with the group
    (8) Drinking is sometimes all right, and sometimes wrong, depending upon the circumstances
    (9) Drinking is all right with parents' approval
    (10) Drinking is all right, if it is properly supervised
    (11) Drinking is all right, at home with parents
    (12) Drinking is wrong, but once to see what it is like is all right
    (13) Drinking is wrong, but it is the individual's own business
    (14) Drinking is never right, no matter what the circumstances.

37. People often talk about types of people because most people in the same occupation and with the same kind of social background have similar habits. Please look at the list of types below, and check *your* opinion of their drinking habits. Be sure to check *only once* for each type.

Type of Person	*Drinks Heavily*	*Drinks Sometimes*	*Drinks Never*	*Don't Know*
Movie stars	....	....	....	....
Television actors	....	....	....	....
Newspaper reporters	....	....	....	....
Book authors (writers)	....	....	....	....
Professional people (lawyers, doctors, etc.)	....	....	....	....
Businessmen	....	....	....	....
College teachers	....	....	....	....
School teachers	....	....	....	....
People like me	....	....	....	....
Leaders in my school (student leaders)	....	....	....	....
School athletes	....	....	....	....
College students	....	....	....	....

Type of Person	Drinks Heavily	Drinks Sometimes	Drinks Never	Don't Know
People who have dropped out of school	....	....	....	....
People who have little money	....	....	....	....
People with average incomes	....	....	....	....
Wealthy people	....	....	....	....
High-school students	....	....	....	....
Religious students	....	....	....	....
Religious people	....	....	....	....

38. Which of the following types of trouble have you had about either drinking or not drinking? Please circle any of the items in the list below which are appropriate.

1. Parents' disapproval
2. My teachers disapprove
3. Getting into trouble with the police
4. The people in my church don't approve
5. Adults criticize me
6. My friends don't like it
7. People think you're a sissy, or chicken
8. People think you're a square
9. People are afraid to confide in me
10. My boyfriend doesn't like me to drink (for girls)
11. My boyfriend wants me to drink (for girls)
12. My girlfriend doesn't want me to drink (for boys)
13. My girlfriend wants me to drink (for boys)
14. Some of the other students disapprove
15. Costs too much to drink
16. Fear of traffic accident
17. Loss of self-control
18. It's bad for health
19. I sometimes think I'd like to try it
20. I am afraid I might not be allowed to play on the team
21. I have poor grades
22. I have trouble keeping my attendance regular
23. It is difficult to get and keep a job
24. Other (list them) ....

Bibliography

1. Bacon, S. D. Inebriety, Social Integration and Marriage. Highland Park, N.J.; Hillhouse Press; 1949.
2. Bacon, S. D. Sociology and the problems of alcohol; foundations for a sociological study of drinking behavior. Quart. J. Stud. Alc. **4:** 402–445, 1943.
3. Bainton, R. H. The churches and alcohol. Quart. J. Stud. Alc. **6:** 45–58, 1945.
4. Bales, R. F. Cultural differences in the rates of alcoholism. Quart. J. Stud. Alc. **6:** 480–499, 1946.
5. Beale, R. The Ethnology of the Western Mixe. (University of California Publications in American Archaeology and Ethnology, No. 42.) Berkeley; University of California Press; 1955.
6. Becker, H. S. and Carper, J. The elements of identification with an occupation. Amer. sociol. Rev. **21:** 341–348, 1956.
7. Benedict, R. The Chrysanthemum and the Sword; Patterns of Japanese Culture. Boston; Houghton Mifflin; 1946.
8. Blake, R. R. and Ramsey, G. V., eds. Perception: An Approach to Personality. New York; Ronald; 1951.
9. Bunzel, R. The role of alcoholism in two Central American cultures. Psychiatry **3:** 361–387, 1940.
10. Cassirer, E. Essay on Man. New York; Doubleday; 1953.
11. Clark, R. A. The projective measurement of experimentally induced levels of sexual motivation. J. exper. Psychol. **44:** 391–399, 1952.
12. Cloward, R. A. and Ohlin, L. E. Delinquency and Opportunity. New York; Free Press; 1960.
13. Cohen, Y. A. Social Structure and Personality. New York; Holt, Rinehart and Winston; 1961.
14. Cottrell, L. S. The analysis of situational fields in social psychology. Amer. sociol. Rev. **7:** 370–382, 1942.
15. Cottrell, L. S. Some neglected problems in social psychology. Amer. sociol. Rev. **15:** 705–712, 1950.
16. Devereux, G. The function of alcohol in Mohave Society. Quart. J. Stud. Alc. **9:** 207–251, 1948.
17. Dollard, J. Drinking mores of the social classes. In: Alcohol, Science and Society; Ch. 8, pp. 95–104. New Haven; Quarterly Journal of Studies on Alcohol; 1945.
18. Eisenstadt, S. N. African age groups; a comparative study. Africa **24** (No. 2): 100–113, 1954.
19. Eisenstadt, S. N. Reference group behavior and social integration; an exploratory study. Amer. sociol. Rev. **19:** 175–185, 1954.

20. EISENSTADT, S. N. From Generation to Generation: Age Groups and Social Structure. New York; Free Press; 1956.
21. ELKIN, F. and WESTLEY, W. A. The myth of adolescent culture. Amer. sociol. Rev. **20**: 680–684, 1955.
22. ERIKSON, E. H. Childhood and Society. New York; Norton; 1950.
23. ERIKSON, E. H. The problem of ego identity. In: STEIN, M. R., VIDICH, A. J. and WHITE, D. M., eds. Identity and Anxiety. New York; Free Press; 1960.
24. ERIKSON, E. H. Youth: fidelity and diversity. Daedalus **91** (Winter): 5–27, 1962.
25. FLEESON, W. and GILDEA, E. F. A study of the personalities of 289 abnormal drinkers. Quart. J. Stud. Alc. **3**: 409–432, 1942.
26. FOOTE, N. Identification as the basis for a theory of motivation. Amer. sociol. Rev. **16**: 14–22, 1951.
27. GLAD, D. D. Attitudes and experiences of American-Jewish and American-Irish male youth as related to differences in adult rates of inebriety. Quart. J. Stud. Alc. **8**: 406–472, 1947.
28. GOFFMAN, E. The Presentation of Self in Everyday Life. New York; Doubleday; 1959.
29. GUSFIELD, J. R. Social structure and moral reform. A study of the Woman's Christian Temperance Union. Amer. J. Sociol. **61**: 221–232, 1955.
30. GUSFIELD, J. R. The structural context of college drinking. Quart. J. Stud. Alc. **22**: 428–443, 1961.
31. HALLOWELL, A. I. Handbook of Psychological Leads for Ethnological Field Workers. (Mimeographed.) Washington, D.C.; Committee on Culture and Personality, National Research Council; 1937.
32. HALLOWELL, A. I. The self and its behavioral environment. In: HALLOWELL, A. I. Culture and Experience. Philadelphia; University of Philadelphia Press; 1955.
33. HAVIGHURST, R. J. Developmental Tasks and Education. Chicago; University of Chicago Press; 1949.
34. HOFSTRA RESEARCH BUREAU, PSYCHOLOGICAL DIVISION, HOFSTRA COLLEGE, N. Y. Use of Alcoholic Beverages by High School Students in Nassau County Related to Parental Permissiveness. New York; Sheppard Foundation; 1954.
35. HOIJER, H. The relation of language to culture. In: KROEBER, A. L., ed. Anthropology Today. Chicago; University of Chicago Press; 1953.
36. HOLLINGSHEAD, A. B. Elmtown's Youth: The Impact of Social Classes on Adolescents. New York; Wiley; 1949.
37. HONIGMANN, J. J. and HONIGMANN, I. Drinking in an Indian-white community. Quart. J. Stud. Alc. **5**: 575–619, 1945.
38. HORTON, D. The functions of alcohol in primitive societies; a cross-cultural survey. Quart. J. Stud. Alc. **4**: 199–320, 1943.
39. HYMAN, H. The value systems of different classes; a social psychological contribution to the analysis of stratification. In: BENDIX, R.

and LIPSET, S. M., eds. Class, Status and Power. New York; Free Press; 1953.

40. JELLINEK, E. M. Phases of alcohol addiction. Quart. J. Stud. Alc. 13: 673–684, 1952.
41. JELLINEK, E. M. The Disease Concept of Alcoholism. Highland Park, N.J.; Hillhouse Press; 1960.
42. KAHL, J. A. and DAVIS, J. A. A comparison of indexes of socio-economic status. Amer. sociol. Rev. **20**: 317–325, 1955.
43. UNIVERSITY OF KANSAS, DEPARTMENT OF SOCIOLOGY AND ANTHROPOLOGY. Attitudes of High School Students Toward Alcoholic Beverages. New York; Sheppard Foundation; 1956.
44. KELLER, M. The definition of alcoholism and the estimation of its prevalence. In: PITTMAN, D. J. and SNYDER, C. R., eds. Society, Culture and Drinking Patterns; Ch. 17, pp. 310-329. New York; Wiley; 1962.
45. KNUPFER, G. Characteristics of Abstainers. A Comparison of Drinkers and Non-Drinkers in a Large California City. (Report No. 3; California Drinking Practices Study.) Berkeley; State of California, Department of Public Health; 1961.
46. LABARRE, W. Some observations on character structure in the Orient. Psychiatry **9**: 375–395, 1946.
47. LANDIS, B. Y. Some economic aspects of inebriety. In: Alcohol, Science and Society; Ch. 15, pp. 201–220. New Haven; Quarterly Journal of Studies on Alcohol; 1945.
48. LANDMAN, R. H. Studies of drinking in Jewish culture: *III*. Drinking patterns of children and adolescents attending religious schools. Quart. J. Stud. Alc. **13**: 87–94, 1952.
49. LEMERT, E. M. Alcohol and the Northwest Coast Indians. (University of California Publications in Culture and Society, Vol. 2, No. 6, pp. 303–406.) Berkeley; University of California Press; 1954.
50. LINDESMITH, A. R. Opiate Addiction. Bloomington, Ind.; Principia Press; 1947.
51. LINTON, R. Age and sex categories. Amer. sociol. Rev. **7**: 589–603, 1942.
52. LINTON, R. The Cultural Background of Personality. New York; Appleton-Century-Croft; 1945.
53. LOLLI, G., SERRIANNI, E., BANISSONI, F., GOLDER, G., MARIANI, A., MCCARTHY, R. G. and TONER, M. The use of wine and other alcoholic beverages by a group of Italians and Americans of Italian extraction. Quart. J. Stud. Alc. **13**: 27–48, 1952.
54. MCCARTHY, R. G. and DOUGLASS, E. M. Instruction on alcohol problems in public schools. Quart. J. Stud. Alc. **8**: 609–635, 1948.
55. MCCARTHY, R. G. and DOUGLASS, E. M. Alcohol and Social Responsibility. New York; Crowell; 1949.
56. MACRORY, B. E. The tavern and the community. Quart. J. Stud. Alc. **13**: 609–637, 1952.

57. MADDOX, G. L. Teenage drinking in the United States. In: PITTMAN, D. J. and SNYDER, C. R., eds. Society, Culture and Drinking Patterns; Ch. 12, pp. 230–245. New York; Wiley; 1962.
58. MAXWELL, M. A. Drinking behavior in the state of Washington. Quart. J. Stud. Alc. **13**: 219–239, 1952.
59. MEAD, M. Male and Female. New York; New American Library; 1955.
60. MERTON, R. K. Social Theory and Social Structure. New York; Free Press; 1950.
61. MERTON, R. K. and KITT, A. S. Some contributions to the theory of reference group behavior. In: MERTON, R. K. and LAZARSFIELD, P. F., eds. Continuities in Social Research. New York; Free Press; 1950.
62. MILLS, C. W. Situated action and vocabularies of motives. Amer. sociol. Rev. **5**: 904–913, 1940.
63. MOORE, W. F. and TUMIN, M. M. Social functions of ignorance. Amer. sociol. Rev. **14**: 787–795, 1949.
64. MULFORD, H. A. and MILLER, D. W. Drinking in Iowa. Sections I-V. Quart. J. Stud. Alc. **20**: 704–726, 1959; **21**: 26–39, 267–278, 279–291, 483–499, 1960.
65. MYERSON, A. Alcohol; a study of social ambivalence. Quart. J. Stud. Alc. **1**: 13–20, 1940.
66. PARSONS, T. An analytical approach to the theory of social stratification. Amer. J. Sociol. **45**: 841–862, 1940.
67. PARSONS, T. Age and sex in the social structure of the United States. Amer. sociol. Rev. **7**: 604–616, 1942.
68. PARSONS, T. The theory of symbolism in relation to action. In: PARSONS, T., BALES, R. F. and SHILS, E., eds. Working Papers in the Theory of Action. New York; Free Press; 1953.
69. PARSONS, T. Youth in the context of American society. Daedalus **91** (Winter): 97–123, 1962.
70. PFAUTZ, H. W. The current literature on social stratification. Critique and bibliography. Amer. J. Sociol. **58**: 391–418, 1953.
71. RILEY, J. W., JR. and MARDEN, C. F. The social pattern of alcoholic drinking. Quart. J. Stud. Alc. **8**: 265–273, 1947.
72. RILEY, J. W., JR., MARDEN, C. F. and LIFSCHITZ, M. The motivational pattern of drinking. Quart. J. Stud. Alc. **9**: 353–362, 1948.
73. SAPIR, E. The status of linguistics as a science. In: MEDELBAUM, D., ed. Selected Writings of Edward Sapir. Berkeley; University of California Press; 1949.
74. SCHILDER, P. The psychogenesis of alcoholism. Quart. J. Stud. Alc. **2**: 277–292, 1941.
75. SHEERE, M. Cognitive theory. In: LINDZEY, G., ed. Handbook of Social Psychology. Cambridge, Mass.; Addison-Wesley; 1954.
76. SKOLNICK, J. H. Religious affiliation and drinking behavior. Quart. J. Stud. Alc. **19**: 452–470, 1958.

77. SLATER, A. D. A study of the use of alcoholic beverages among high school students in Utah. Quart. J. Stud. Alc. **13**: 78–86, 1952.
78. SNEIDLER, M. B. and RAVITZ, M. J. A Jewish peer group. Amer. J. Sociol. **61**: 11–15, 1955.
79. SNYDER, C. L. Alcohol and the Jews. A Cultural Study of Drinking and Sobriety. (Monographs of the Rutgers Center of Alcohol Studies, No. 1.) New Brunswick; Publications Division, Rutgers Center of Alcohol Studies; and New York; Free Press; 1958.
80. STONE, G. P. and FORM, W. H. Instabilities in status: the problems of hierarchy in the community study of status arrangements. Amer. sociol. Rev. **18**: 149–162, 1953.
81. STOUFFER, S. A. An analysis of conflicting norms. Amer. sociol. Rev. **14**: 707–718, 1949.
82. STRAUS, R. and BACON, S. D. Drinking in College. New Haven; Yale University Press; 1953.
83. STRECKER, E. A. Chronic alcoholism; a psychological survey. Quart. J. Stud. Alc. **2**: 12–17, 1941.
84. SUMNER, W. G. Folkways. Boston; Ginn; 1906.
85. TABA, H. Moral beliefs and the ability to apply them in solving problems of conduct. In: HAVIGHURST, R. J. and TABA, H., eds. Adolescent Character and Personality. New York; Wiley; 1949.
86. THOMAS, W. I. The Child in America. New York; Knopf; 1929.
87. THOMPSON, G. N. A psychiatric formulation of alcoholism. Quart. J. Stud. Alc. **7**: 346–355, 1946.
88. WARNER, H. S., MCPEEK, F. W. and JELLINEK, E. M. Philosophy of the temperance movement: a panel discussion. In: Alcohol, Science and Society; Ch. 19, pp. 267–285. New Haven; Quarterly Journal of Studies on Alcohol; 1945.
89. WARNER, L., MEEKER, M. and EELLS, K. Social class in America. Chicago; Science Research Associates; 1949.
90. WASHBURNE, C. Primitive Drinking. A Study of the Uses and Functions of Alcohol in Preliterate Societies. New Haven; College and University Press; 1961.
91. WATTENBERG, W. W. and MOIR, J. B. Teen Age Drinkers. Lansing; Social Science Research Center, Wayne University; 1955.
92. WEBER, M. Class, status and party. In: BENDIX, R. and LIPSET, S. M., eds. Class, Status and Power. New York; Free Press; 1953.
93. WHORF, B. L. The relation of habitual thought and behavior to language. In: SPIER, L., HALLOWELL, A. I. and NEWMAN, S. S., eds. Language, Culture and Personality. Menasha, Wis.; Sapir Memorial Publication Fund; 1941.
94. WILLIAMS, R. M. American Society. New York; Knopf; 1952.
95. UNIVERSITY OF WISCONSIN, BUREAU OF ECONOMICS, SOCIOLOGY AND ANTHROPOLOGY. Attitudes of High School Students toward Alcoholic Beverages. New York; Sheppard Foundation; 1956.

Index of Names

Index of Subjects